On Ceasing to Be Human

On Ceasing to Be Human

Gerald L. Bruns

STANFORD UNIVERSITY PRESS
STANFORD, CALIFORNIA

Stanford University Press
Stanford, California

© 2011 by the Board of Trustees of the Leland Stanford Junior University.
All rights reserved.

No part of this book may be reproduced or transmitted in any form or by any means, electronic or mechanical, including photocopying and recording, or in any information storage or retrieval system without the prior written permission of Stanford University Press.

Printed in the United States of America on acid-free, archival-quality paper

Library of Congress Cataloging-in-Publication Data

Bruns, Gerald L.
 On ceasing to be human / Gerald L. Bruns.
  p. cm.
 Includes bibliographical references and index.
 ISBN 978-0-8047-7208-2 (cloth : alk. paper) — ISBN 978-0-8047-7209-9 (pbk. : alk. paper)
 1. Human beings—Philosophy. 2. Continental philosophy—France. 3. Philosophy, Modern—20th century. I. Title.
 BD450.B75 2011
 128—dc22

                              2010016752

Designed by Bruce Lundquist
Typeset at Stanford University Press in 9/15 Palatino with Walbaum display

For Joe Buttigieg

Contents

Acknowledgments	ix
Abbreviations	xi
Prologue: On the Freedom of Non-Identity	1
Otherwise Than Human (Toward Sovereignty)	13
What Is Human Recognition? (On Zones of Indistinction)	31
Desubjectivation (Michel Foucault's Aesthetics of Experience)	47
Becoming Animal (Some Simple Ways)	61
Derrida's Cat (Who Am I?)	79
Notes	99
Works Cited	119
Index	133

Acknowledgments

This book developed over the years in many different ways, starting perhaps with my reading in the early 1980s of the fourth part of Stanley Cavell's *The Claim of Reason*, with its worries about "the precariousness of human identity," which resonated at crucial moments with my long-standing interest in the work of Maurice Blanchot, for whom an identity of any sort is a dubious possession. Likewise I recall my years in the English Department at Notre Dame and our informal reading groups made up of faculty and students interested in the vexed relations between philosophy and literature. We often spent our time in slow, patient readings of difficult texts by European thinkers (Levinas, Foucault, Derrida) for whom the singularity of things eludes the concepts and categories in which we try to contain them. I remember with special warmth Jim Hansen, Erich Hertz, Grant Jenkins, and Ewa and Krys Ziarek. A pilot study of sorts, bearing this book's title, was presented as the Roger Allan Moore Lecture at the School for Social Medicine, the Harvard Medical School, in April of 1998. I'm very grateful to Dr. Arthur Kleinman for his invitation to present the lecture, and for his and his wife Joan's warm hospitality. The writing of this book was substantially completed during 2007–8 when I was a Marta Sutton Weeks Faculty Fellow at the Stanford Humanities Center. My thanks to John Bender, then director of the Center, and to the Center's marvelous staff, especially Robert Barrick, Matthew Tiews, and Nicole Coleman. I'm grateful to R. M. Berry, Jr., and Herman Rapaport for their careful reading of the manuscript and for their helpful suggestions for revision. Special thanks to Gary Gutting for his help with the chapter on Michel Foucault.

This book is for Joe Buttigieg, my friend and colleague of twenty-five years, in memory of the courses we taught together, our many conversations and spirited disagreements, and (not the least) our hilarity at the absurdities of academic life.

Abbreviations

Giorgio Agamben
HS   *Homo Sacer: Sovereign Power and Bare Life*
IH   *Infancy and History: On the Destruction of Experience*
O   *The Open: Man and Animal*

Karl Ameriks and Dieter Sturma, eds.
MS   *The Modern Subject: Conceptions of the Self in Classical German Philosophy*

Antonin Artaud
AA   *Antonin Artaud: Selected Writings*

Georges Bataille
AS   *The Accursed Share: An Essay on General Economy*, vols. 2–3
ExI   *L'expérience intérieure*
IE   *Inner Experience*
VE   *Visions of Excess: Selected Writings, 1927–1939*

Maurice Blanchot
DH   *Le dernier homme*
LM   *The Last Man*
EI   *L'entretien infini*
IC   *The Infinite Conversation*
EL   *L'espace littéraire*
SL   *The Space of Literature*
F   *Friendship*

xii *Abbreviations*

PD   *Le pas au-delà*
SNB *The Step Not Beyond*

Stanley Cavell
CR   *The Claim of Reason: Wittgenstein, Skepticism, Morality, and Tragedy*
CH   *Conditions Handsome and Unhandsome: The Constitution of Emersonian Perfectionism*

Simon Critchley and Peter Dews, eds.
DS   *Deconstructed Subjectivities*

Gilles Deleuze
FB   *Francis Bacon: The Logic of Sensation*

Gilles Deleuze and Félix Guattari
AO   *Anti-Oedipus: Capitalism and Schizophrenia*
MP   *Mille plateaux*
TP   *A Thousand Plateaus*

Jacques Derrida
LAN *L'animal que donc je suis*
ANT *The Animal That I Therefore Am*
WC   *"'Eating Well,' or the Calculation of the Subject: An Interview with Jacques Derrida"*
ON   *On the Name*

Jacques Derrida and Maurizio Ferraris
TS   *A Taste for the Secret*

Michel Foucault
DEI *Dits et écrits, I: 1954–1976*
DEII *Dits et écrits, II: 1976–1988*

E	*Essential Works of Foucault, 1954–1984*, vol. 1: *Ethics, Subjectivity, and Truth*
A	*Essential Works of Foucault: 1954–1984*, vol 2: *Aesthetics, Method, and Epistemology*
P	*Essential Works of Michel Foucault, 1954–1984*, vol. 3: *Power*
HSI	*Histoire de la sexualité, I: La volonté de savoir*
HSII	*Histoire de la sexualité, II: L'usage des plaisirs*
HSIII	*Histoire de la sexualité, III: Le souci de soi*
VS	*The History of Sexuality*, vol. 1: *An Introduction*
UP	*The History of Sexuality*, vol. 2: *The Uses of Pleasure*
CS	*The History of Sexuality*, vol. 3: *The Care of the Self*
AS	*L'archéologie du savoir*
AK	*The Archeology of Knowledge*
FD	*Folie et déraison: Histoire de la folie à l'âge classique*
MC	*Madness and Civilization: A History of Insanity in the Age of Reason*
NC	*Naissance de la clinique*
BC	*The Birth of the Clinic: An Archeology of Medical Perception*
OT	*The Order of Things: An Archeology of the Human Sciences*
SP	*Surveiller et punir: Naissance de la prison*
DP	*Discipline and Punish: The Birth of the Prison*

Franz Kafka

KCS	*The Complete Stories*

Emmanuel Levinas

AE	*Autrement qu'être ou au-delà de l'essence*
OTB	*Otherwise Than Being, or Beyond Essence*
CPP	*Collected Philosophical Papers*
DF	*Difficult Freedom: Essays in Judaism*
TeI	*Totalité et infini*
TI	*Totality and Infinity*

Jean-François Lyotard
I   *The Inhuman: Reflections on Time*

Jean-Luc Nancy
BP   *The Birth to Presence*
CD   *La communauté désœuvrée*
InC   *The Inoperative Community*
ESP   *Être singulier pluriel*
BSP   *Being Singular Plural*
ExL   *L'expérience de la liberté*
EF   *The Experience of Freedom*
TS   *Tombe de sommeil*
FS   *The Fall of Sleep*

Jean-Paul Sartre
BN   *Being and Nothingness*

Michel Tournier
V   *Vendredi, ou les limbes du Pacifique*
F   *Friday*

Auguste Villiers de l'Isle-Adam
TE   *Tomorrow's Eve*

On Ceasing to Be Human

Prologue

ON THE FREEDOM OF NON-IDENTITY

> When to write is to discover the interminable, the writer who enters this region does not leave himself behind in order to approach the universal. He does not move toward a surer world, a finer or better justified world where everything would be ordered according to the clarity of the impartial. He does not discover the admirable language which speaks honorably for all. What speaks in him is the fact that, in one way or another, he is no longer himself; he isn't anyone any more.
> —Maurice Blanchot, "The Essential Solitude"

The French writer Maurice Blanchot belongs to an anarchic tradition in which writing is neither the expression nor construction of anything, nor a transport to a higher (or nether) world; instead it is a kind of limit-experience in which the one who writes is turned inside out, evacuated, becoming something entirely other, without identity. Blanchot frequently figures this event as a movement from "I" to "he," which in French is a form of neutralization where the pronoun *il* is indeterminately "he/it," neither one nor the other: "The third person," he says, "is myself become no one" (*EL*, 23/*SL*, 28).[1] Imagine being no one, without properties or attributes, inaccessible to predication.

The paradox is that, for Blanchot, this disappearance of the first person is not a merely negative event; on the contrary, the privations of subjectivity or self-identity constitute a condition of freedom from the logical (not to say social and cultural) order of concepts and rules, categories and distinctions, schemes and types—freedom above all from the polarities of sameness and difference or the one and the many. In an important essay, "The Relation of the Third Kind (Man Without Horizon)," Blanchot writes: "Even more than Being, even more than the Same, the Rigor of the One holds thought captive."[2] Nor is it just thought that is confined or fixed by the One: whatever exists, its singularity, irreducibility, and strangeness, disappears beneath a concept—think of the word "Man" in this respect. Blanchot's "man without horizon" is decontextualized, no longer (to speak strictly) human. That is, the horizonless figure serves Blanchot as a way of addressing the alterity of both oneself and others, unconditioned by the conceptual frames of genus, species, or any form of denomination. Even speaking of one's *self* is for Blanchot saying too much. In *The Step Not Beyond* Blanchot writes: "The self is not a self but the same [*le même du moi-même*], not some personal, impersonal identity, sure and vacillating, but the law or rule that conventionally assures the ideal identity of terms and notations. The self is therefore an abbreviation that one could call canonical, a formula that regulates and, if you like, blesses, in the first person, the pretention of the same to primacy."[3] The self is not something I possess; it is a regulatory concept that keeps the "I" in line like a number in a sequence or a slot in a hierarchy. Or, as Blanchot sometimes expresses it: "loss of self, anonymity, loss of sovereignty" is also the loss "of all subordination."[4]

Being *insubordinate* to the rule of identity or primacy of the same is likewise a major theme in Emmanuel Levinas's ethical theory.[5] In his essay "Substitution," Levinas speaks of a "finite freedom" in contrast to the unconditional autonomy that Kant, for example, attributed to the cognitive subject, who is unconstrained in his initiatives except by the laws of reason of which he is the original legislator (supposing "he" to be the word).[6] For Levinas, my relation to others—my responsibility for the good of the other—is on the hither (anarchic) side of any initiatives that I might undertake (or not) in their behalf; that is, it is prior to any morality or ethics that would prescribe my duties toward my fellows—and justify me in the event that I fulfill these prescriptions. As an ethical subject I am no longer at one with myself but have from the start been overtaken by the claims the other has on me—*substituted*, as Levinas likes to express it, one for the other, so that the other is closer to me than I am to myself. "Subjectivity," Levinas says, "is structured as the other in the same [*le Autre-dans-le-Même*]" (*AE*, 46/*OTB*, 25). The paradox—which is symmetrical with Blanchot's paradox—is that substitution is not alienation but is an "anarchic liberation":

> Substitution frees the subject from ennui, that is, from the enchainment to itself, where the ego [*Moi*] suffocates in itself [*en Soi*] due to the tautological way of identity, and ceaselessly seeks after the distraction of games and sleep in a movement than never wears out. This liberation is not an action, a commencement, nor any vicissitude of essence and of ontology, where the equality with oneself would be established in the form of self-consciousness. An anarchic liberation, it emerges, without being assumed, without turning into a beginning, in inequality with oneself. (*AE*, 198/*OTB*, 124)

Inequality with oneself: whereas Blanchot thinks of writing as a movement toward the neutral third person (*il*: he/it), Levinas thinks of the ethical relation (or, as he sometimes prefers, "election") as a movement from "I" to "me." He writes: "Consciousness, knowing of oneself by oneself, is not all there is to subjectivity. It already rests on a 'subjective condition,' an identity that one calls ego or I. It is true that, when asking about the meaning of this identity, we have the habit either of denouncing in it a reified substance, or of finding in it once again the for-itself [*pour soi*] of consciousness. In the traditional teaching of idealism, subject and consciousness are equivalent concepts. The *who* or the *me* [*le qui ou l'un*] are not even suspected" (*AE*, 162/*OTB*, 102–3).[7]

What is it to be a *who* or a *me* or, even more radically, a *no one*: without identity, that is, no longer able to say "I"? One answer, says Jean-Luc Nancy, is to be found (of all places) in *sleep*, where consciousness and subjectivity become empty concepts. In *The Fall of Sleep* he writes: "I sleep and this *I* that sleeps can no more say it sleeps than that it could say that it is dead. So it is another who sleeps in my place.... It is that entire other who I am as soon as I am removed from all aspects of me and from all my functions except the function of sleeping, which is perhaps not a function, or else functions only to suspend all functioning."⁸ Wisely Nancy does not try to give sleep a definition, nor is his account a phenomenological analysis, because sleep is not phenomenal, nor is the one who sleeps the subject of an experience, since subjectivity, self, and identity are precisely what sleep puts to rest:

> The sleeping *self* [*soi*] does not appear: it is not phenomenalized. . . . Sleep does not authorize the analysis of any form of appearance whatsoever, since it shows itself to itself as this appearance that appears only as non-appearing, as returning all appearing on itself and in itself, allowing the waking phenomenologist approaching the bed to perceive nothing but the appearance of its disappearance, the attestation of its retreat. (*TS*, 30/*FS*, 13)

Of course, the sleeper dreams, but not the way the *cogito* thinks: "'I am,' murmured by the unconsciousness of a dreamer, testifies less to an 'I' strictly conceived than to a 'self' simply withdrawn into itself, out of reach of any questioning and of any representation. Murmured by unconsciousness, 'I am' becomes unintelligible" (*TS*, 31–32/*FS*, 14). One might as well say, *no one sleeps*—"The man or woman whose mouth thus mumbles a confused attestation of existence is no longer 'I' and is not truly 'self': but beyond the two, or simply set apart, indifferent to any kind of ipseity [*ipseity*: individual identity]" (*TS*, 32/*FS*, 14).

Yet for all of that, sleep is not a confinement but freedom from, among other things, insomnia, which is a condition of exposure to the night:

> Ambulances tear through the night, and cannons, and rocket launchings, children crying, tanks rumbling, rending pains in the chest, in the bellies of the cancerous or the wounded, harsh light of lamps that one cannot or will not turn off, obsessive thoughts, torments, remorse, feverish anticipations, fears— fears more than anything else, fears of everything. (*TS*, 71/*FS*, 37)

Or perhaps it is exposure to the day's (or the world's) invasion:

> The figures that the day arranges for recognition rise up again from the darkness disguised in evil masks, the thoughts we know how to manage carefully burst into anxieties, suffocations, aporias that close over onto themselves as long as day has not dissolved them. Night engenders terror, obsession, ravage,

and panic. It is not a matter of an insomnia that wanders from sleep itself, its transformation into a wakefulness deprived of day, into a glowing nightlight whose gleam maintains the agitation of the soul with a clear awareness of sleep usurped, split open, transformed into its twofold awakening. On the contrary, it is a matter of the world in which it is impossible to sleep, of the world in which it is forbidden to sleep because of a process of torture whose effectiveness is not in doubt. (*TS*, 71–72/*FS*, 38)

Nancy wonders whether this is not what our world has come to—he imagines a dystopia (looking for all the world like the twentieth and now twenty-first centuries), in which sleepers are "harassed, always on the alert, less fallen asleep than thrown into sleep, precipitated by numbness from short hours broken by knocking sounds in the head, knocks on the door, blows or gunshots. Sleepers not so much sleeping as knocked out, conquered at night as they were during in the day, piled into camps or lying in ditches, in trucks or in skiffs, hunted, chased from their hurried repose" (*TS*, 73/*FS*, 38–39).

In this dystopia (where one's papers are never in order) the deprivation of sleep and the deprivation of freedom are of a piece, joined at the hip. But freedom here is perhaps freedom of a kind for which we lack a theory—the lack of which, moreover, might well teach us something about freedom.

Earlier, in a particularly recondite essay entitled "Identity and Trembling," Nancy wrote: "Sleep, perhaps, has never been philosophical."[9] The reason is that philosophy, at least since Hegel, has always conceived human subjectivity in terms of self-consciousness or the self-identity of the spirit.[10] But subjectivity in this sense is the product of negation: "No more than it can die—nor more than it can 'seriously' die, if we can say that with a straight face—can the subject be born, or can it sleep. Immortal, unengendered, insomniac: this is the triple negation over which the life of the spirit rises, imperturbably adult and awake" (*BP*, 12). For Nancy self-conscious spirit, if it is anything at all, is not all there is. There is also that which is capable of being affected—capable of feeling and, among other things, capable of sleep. And in defiance of Hegel (and of most philosophers one can think of) Nancy does not hesitate to call this the "soul." The soul is simply you and me, each in our own singularity, falling (as we doze off) beneath the threshold of philosophical description. For Hegel, to be human is to be in a position of avid surveillance from which nothing can hide—which is why, as Nancy says, Hegel was so troubled by the pathology of hypnosis ("magnetic somnambulism"), in which the spirit is, to all appearances, awake but no longer self-identical—and, above all, no longer free. As Nancy says:

> The freedom that speculative spirit grasps is self-determined, and so sublates all determination. Yet determination *itself* is first grasped not in autonomy but in heteronomy. Could freedom, like magnetic sleep, be given by another? Speculative spirit prefers not to think so, cannot think so. It designates heteronomy as pathology. But in pathology, an insurmountable—and perhaps constitutive—affection of its own freedom stymies it, fascinates it.
>
> Not that hypnotism should be thought of as a liberating force. . . . But this means that philosophical speculation about "pathology," and the general determination of affected being as "pathology," both depend directly on thinking of freedom as the pure self-positing and pure self-production of waking consciousness. Ultimately, the soul's sleep would require another thinking of freedom. (*BP*, 21)

All by itself, the sense of the question, "Could freedom . . . be given by another?" is far from clear, but "another thinking of freedom"—a *finite* thinking that no longer depends on concepts of consciousness or the self-possessed spirit, or indeed that no longer depends on concepts at all—is what Nancy pursues in *The Experience of Freedom*.[11] Freedom here is not the property of a subject but rather belongs to existence at the level of its singularity, irreducibility, and irrepressibility. Nancy calls it "the free determination of existence":

> This free determination (whose formulation might well be only a tautology) is not the diffraction of a principle, nor the multiple effect of a cause, but is the an-archy—the origin removed from every logic of origin, from every archeology—of a singular and thus in essence plural arising whose being *as being* is

neither ground, nor element, nor reason, but truth, which would amount to saying, under the circumstances, freedom. (*ExL*, 16–17/*EF*, 13)[12]

Note the phrase: "the an-archy . . . of the singular."[13] Freedom is, in effect, the excess of things with respect to any determination, their anarchy with respect to any principle or rule. Nancy speaks of freedom in terms of "generosity" and "prodigality"; freedom bears, he says, "the values of impulse, chance, luck, the unforeseen. . . . Also: laughter, tears, scream, word, rapture, chill, shock, energy, sweetness" (*ExL*, 79/*EF*, 56):

> It is a bursting [*éclat*] or a singularity of existence, which means existence deprived of essence and delivered to this inessentiality, to its own surprise as well as to its own decision, to its own indecision as well as to its own generosity. But this "own" of freedom is nothing subjective; it is the inappropriable burst from which the very existence of the subject comes to the subject, with no support in existence, and even without a relation to it, being "itself" more singularly than any ipseity, "itself" in the burst of a "there exists" that nothing founds or necessitates, that happens unexpectedly and only surprises, vertiginous to the point that it is no longer even a question of assigning an "abyss" to its vertigo: this very vertigo, its existence and its thought are the vertigo of the prodigality that makes it exist *without allotting it any essence* and that is therefore not an essence, but rather the free burst of being. (*ExL*, 81/*EF*, 57–58)

One cannot help noticing the decorum here between the prodigality of freedom and Nancy's prodigal, prodigious prose, which elaborates and embellishes its theme without ever really defining it (bursting the seams of the propositional style of philosophical thinking). Indeed, earlier in his book Nancy asks whether in fact philosophy is free to speak about freedom at all, and his answer is *no*, it is not: the philosopher cannot speak of "*freedom* as such—he can only associate a motif, but not assemble a concept or an Idea (or he can renounce freedom by taking refuge in the ineffable . . .)" (*ExL*, 43/*EP*3).

Neither can philosophy speak about whatever it is that enjoys freedom— modern art, poetry, and music come to mind ("The aim of every artistic utopia today," Theodor Adorno writes, "is to make things in ignorance of what they are").[14] Nancy prefers more mundane things—laughter being another example besides sleep. In his essay "Laughter, Presence," Nancy writes:

> Laughter always bursts—and loses itself in its peals. As soon as it bursts out, it is lost to all appropriation, to all presentation. This loss is neither funny nor sad; it is not serious, and it is not a joke. We always *make* too much of laughter, we overload it with meaning or nonsense, we take it to the point of tears or to the revelation of nothingness. But laughter bursts—laughter, which is never *one*, never an essence of laughter, nor the laughter of an essence. (*BP*, 168)

As it happens, the laughter that prompted Nancy to speak about laughter is the laughter of a prostitute in a poem by Baudelaire ("Le désir de peindre" [The Desire to Paint]), and it is this "aesthetic" context that prompts Nancy to speak of "the arts" with the same reserve or finitude that he brings to sleep and freedom (as well as to that hoary old philosophical term, "presence"):

> The arts cannot be represented one by way of another—and they never cease to pass into each other, to present themselves in place of one another. For none of them represents anything. Each of the arts is merely the coming into presence of *some* presence, which thereby models itself. Not of presence in general, nor of the essence of presence. Presence is without essence: this might be what, for want of being said, is laughed by the poem. Some presence, some presences: multiple singularities, which are only present for being singular, and thus multiple, which don't come from any empyrean of presence. Presence "itself" only takes place in the difference of its presences—and each of them only stems from a singular *coming* into presence, a passage through which presence disappears in offering itself. (*BP*, 389)

"Presence is without essence": it does not belong to the order of representation or conceptual clarification. Instead Nancy speaks of "some presence, some presences: multiple singularities."

For Nancy, "multiple singularities" make up all there is. It is what he tries to capture in the oxymoronic phrase "being singular plural," which is (in so many words) how we are with one another—supposing we know "who we are," which is, once more, supposing too much. In one of his texts Nancy puts it plainly: "'We,' now, is non-identical. We no longer have centers. We no longer address one another by way of substance or subject."[15] So how are "we" with one another? In *Being Singular Plural*, Nancy takes Heidegger's concept of *Mitsein*, being-with, in a number of different directions, one of which addresses the question of the relation, not between "myself" and "another," but between singularities—between the multiple "someones" (and also, as it happens, the "somethings") that make up the world.[16] "A single being," Nancy says, "is a contradiction in terms" (*ESP*, 30/*BSP*, 12). There is only "the sharing of a world" (*ESP*, 49/*BSP*, 29), a "being-together" of singularities—except that this "being-together" does not take the form of a composition or unity. Being-together is contiguous rather than continuous; it is a spacing or a "between" rather than a Heideggerian gathering into a holistic community. As Nancy says, "the question has to be posed as to whether being-together can do without a figure and, as a result, without identification, if the whole of its 'substance' consists solely of its spacing" (*ESP*, 67/*BSP*, 47):

> Today, when thinking moves too quickly, when it is fearful and reactionary, it declares that the most commonly recognized forms of identification are indispensable and claim that the destinies proper to them are used up or perverted, whether it be: "people," "nation," "church," or "culture," not to be mention the confused "ethnicity" or the tortuous "roots." There is a whole panorama of membership and property, here, whose political and philosophical history has yet to be written: it is the history of the representation-of-self as the determining element of an originary concept of society. (*ESP*, 67–68/*BSP*, 47)

It is "the history of the representation-of-self as the determining element of an originary concept of society" that Nancy had earlier tried to put behind him in *The Inoperative Community*, where he proposes that there is "nothing to say" about community: "we should not seek a word or a concept for it, but rather recognize in the thought of community a theoretical excess (or, more precisely, an excess in relation to the theoretical) that would oblige us to adopt another *praxis* of discourse and community" (*CD*, 66/*InC*, 25–26). Accordingly, and characteristically, he took recourse to a *via negativa*; for example, a community is *not* any sort of edifice or construction: "Community cannot arise from the domain of *work*. . . . Community necessarily takes place in what Blanchot has called 'unworking' [*désœuvrement*], referring to that which, before or beyond the work, withdraws from the work, and which, no longer having to do with either the production or the completion, encounters interruption, fragmentation, suspension" (*CD*, 78–79/*InC*, 31). Community, Nancy wrote, is a sharing (*partage*), not of something held in common like a set of beliefs or a national identity, but of something passed from one hand to another like a greeting or the opportunity to speak—or a touch. There is "no entity or hypostasis of community because this sharing, this passage, cannot be completed. Incompletion is its 'principle,' taking the term 'incompletion' in an active sense, however, as designating not insufficiency or lack, but the activity of sharing, the dynamic, if you will, of an uninterrupted passage through singular ruptures" (*CD*, 87/*InC*, 35). Sharing is, in this respect, anarchic precisely because it resists the reduction of human relations to the immanent communion of a coherent body or intersubjective relationship. ("Only the fascist masses tend to annihilate community in the delirium of incarnated communion" [*CD*, 87/*InC*, 35].) Community, Nancy says, "is resistance itself: namely, resistance to immanence . . . to all the forms and all the violences of subjectivity" (*CD*, 88/*InC*, 35). So community must be understood in terms of events and movements rather than in terms of structures and meanings. Concepts of a cause or a struggle have greater application to the *partage* of community than do concepts of law, contracts, beliefs, ideals, or national spirit. It is easier to share a pleasure—a laugh or a meal—than a space, frame, or category.

Just so, we may imagine community as a circle that cannot be closed and from which nothing can be excluded, in which case it is uncertain as to how or whether one can any longer speak of a *human* community: "It is not obvious that the community of singularities is limited to 'man' and excludes, for example, the 'animal' (even in the case of 'man' it is not a fortiori certain that this community concerns only 'man' and not also the 'inhuman' or the 'superman,' or, for example, if I may say so with and without a certain *Witz*, 'woman': after all, the difference between sexes is itself a singularity in the difference of singularities)" (*CD*, 71/*InC*, 28). On the contrary, the point is to free the concept of community—or, more exactly, to free you and me—from any denomination, including that of the epithet "human": "in the true movement of community, in the inflection (in the conjugation, in the diction) that articulates it, what is at stake is never humanity, but always *the end of humanity* [*de la fin de l'homme*]. The end of humanity does not mean its goal or culmination. It means something quite different, namely, the limit that man alone can reach, and in reaching it, where he can stop being human, all too human [*d'être simplement humain, trop humain*]" (*CD*, 190/*InC*, 77).

1

Otherwise Than Human

(TOWARD SOVEREIGNTY)

"Man Is a History and Has No Other Nature"
In our present intellectual climate (and indeed for a long time now) it appears that what we call being *human*, human subjectivity, my relation to myself (and to others), being *me* (or not)—these things, whatever they are, are without substance within most of our perspectives, whether conceptual or empirical, meaning that for philosophical and scientific research the concept of the human is either empty, or should be made so. The human has become a mythological or poetic concept, like Heidegger's "gods and mortals," easily replaceable by more up-to-date fictions ("We are all cyborgs now," says Donna Haraway: anthropology gives way to anthropotechnology).[1] The French philosopher Jean-François Lyotard puts it neatly when he says that in our time the task of reason is "to make philosophy inhuman," as if this were to be a kind of second-order secularization.[2] In the introduction to a collection of his essays entitled *The Inhuman*, Lyotard frames two questions: "What if human beings, in humanism's sense, were in the process of becoming inhuman? And what if what is 'proper' to humankind were to be inhabited by the inhuman?"[3]

What could these questions mean? Possibly no more than what social constructionists mean when they cite Michel Foucault's famous line—"Man is an invention of recent date. And one perhaps nearing its end."[4] Or perhaps they mean whatever eliminative materialists mean when they say that the concepts of folk psychology—consciousness, desire, feeling, self, and so on—are scientifically useless and should be got rid of.[5] The philosopher Cora Diamond says—and thinks of herself as alone in contesting the idea—that in our philosophical culture the human is at most a biological concept, or alternatively is no more than an information-processing device, that is, one kind of intentional system among many others; the category of the human as such is no longer of any philosophical or moral interest.[6] Rather like madness (in its old, preclinical sense). But possibly the "end of man" is only what philosophers have always meant by their arguments or intimations that doing philosophy, being philosophical, is incompatible with being (merely) human. In Western culture the human is a border of self-transcendence but otherwise nothing in itself. "Can a human being be free of human nature?" asks Stanley Cavell. Perhaps only by becoming a monster, where the most monstrous thing is a being that looks human but turns out not to be.[7] As Daniel Dennett says, for all you know "some of your best friends may be zombies."[8]

Of course, Cavell must be thinking of someone like Socrates, barefoot in the snow, standing for hours in meditation without the slightest bother, drinking the night through without getting drunk, spending the night in bed with the most beautiful man in Athens without getting an erection.[9] In Plato's *Phaedo* philosophy as *ascesis* is explicitly a disciplined emancipation from human finitude, a kind of virtual death. Modern analytic philosophy, with its logical obsessions, its desire that things should match their concepts, and its despair over the failure of things to do so, is ascetic in much the same way. Cavell thinks that "there is inherent in philosophy a certain drive to the inhuman, to a certain inhuman idea of intellectuality, or of completion, or of the systematic; and that exactly because it is a drive to the inhuman, it is somehow itself the most inescapably human of motivations."[10] Recall Hegel's account of the violence that consciousness inflicts on itself in order to transform itself into Spirit (*Geist*)—a task that requires it to rid itself of everything that is not itself, including perhaps its human embodiment.[11] After all, what happens when the task of *Aufhebung* is finished? In his lectures during the 1930s on the *Phenomenology of Spirit*, Alexandre Kojève extracted from Hegel a famous thesis: "At the end of history man disappears"—but not to worry, he adds in a footnote, this is not "a cosmic catastrophe: the natural World remains what it has been from all eternity. And therefore, it is not a biological catastrophe either: Man remains alive as animal in *harmony* with Nature as given Being. What disappears is Man properly so-called—that is Action negating the given, and Error, or in general the Subject opposed to the Object."[12] At the end of history we are at last free to enjoy our animal satisfactions.

But what is "Man properly so-called," especially since he has begun to replicate himself? In an essay entitled "Machines as Persons?" Christopher Cherry writes: "It is virtually certain that machines which are on the face of it indistinguishable from human beings (and, doubtless, other creatures) will come on the scene sooner rather than later."[13] Whenever they arrive, before as much as after, the major question will be: How should we treat these imitation humans? "The pressures to call them 'persons,'" Cherry says, "will be immense" (23)—and (he says) should be resisted on the grounds that if we begin to identify with these imitation humans we are likely to suffer a leveling that will leave us in a state of ontological indeterminacy (aliquids, whatchamacallits: neither human nor nonhuman but inhuman, or better—since the term "inhuman" is a moral concept that refers to acts of cruelty, of which animals are, according to tradition, incapable—*a*human; but who is "we"?).[14] Cherry proposes that we treat machine-persons the way we treat fictional characters in plays or novels (23). Would this be humane? The philosopher Daniel Dennett thinks that it would not. After all, we (humans) are ourselves, he says, "the direct descendents of . . . self-replicating robots," that is, micromolecular systems of a certain complexity.[15] Dennett would side with Hilary Putnam's argument that the question of whether machine-persons are in some sense conscious or alive "calls for a decision rather than a discovery," and that now would be a good time (but of course he proposed this more than thirty years ago) to raise the question, "Should robots have civil rights?"[16] (And, of course, if robots, why not other creatures as well? Animal rights advocates like Peter Singer have for a long time been well ahead of this question.)[17]

Other than Me

Would these "rights" be the Rights of Man? The French philosopher Emmanuel Levinas remarks that the concept of the "Rights of Man" entails the paradox of the absolute alterity of every person. The human is what is refractory to categories and distinctions of every order, including the humanity of every humanism: "Each man is the only one of his kind" (as if "man" were the word); there is no essence of man or human nature or human species. The human is the absolutely other as such (*Autrui*): "non-interchangeable, incomparable, unique, and irreproducible."[18] As in Plato's *Parmenides*—this is the late Plato who seems to have abandoned the theory of Forms—we are the others of each other, not of any One.[19] So we cannot be contained within a logic of identity or of exclusion or any bivalent (either/or) logic. The problem with humanism, Levinas thinks, is that with respect to human alterity, "it is not sufficiently human" (*AE*, 203/*OTB*, 128). Humanism is concerned chiefly with the productive autonomy of the ego and the self-transparency of a consciousness exercising rational control.[20] In an essay on "Humanism and Anarchy," Levinas says that since Descartes and Kant—that is, in the philosophical culture of modernity—"man" is chiefly the name for the logical subject of objectifying consciousness, the representational-calculative "I" that produces an order of "anonymous structures" in which the human being as a singular and irreducible creature remains invisible.[21] Levinas writes: "As a setting into place of intelligible structures subjectivity can have no internal finality. We are witnessing the ruin of the myth of man [as] an end in himself, and the appearance of an order that is neither human nor nonhuman, one that is, indeed, ordered across man and across the civilizations he is said to have produced, but ordered in the last analysis by the properly rational force of the dialectical or logico-formal system" (*CPP*, 130).[22] As if the "human" subject were simply the indeterminate medium ("neither human nor nonhuman") of a cybernetic or rule-governed rationality: a thinking thing, as Descartes figured it, with no need of a body.

By contrast, for Levinas, and for a number of his contemporaries in European philosophy, the human at the level of the singular—that is, "prior to the distinction between the particular and the universal" (*AE*, 130/*OTB*, 108)—is not a *what* but a *who*; it is not the nominative *I* (*Je*) but the accusative *me* (*moi*).[23] The logical subject of cognition, rational deliberation, justified true beliefs, and conduct beyond reproach—this subject is pure spirit, and is purely theoretical. The *who* or the *me* by contrast is corporeal, made of flesh or skin; it exists as a mode of sensibility or exposure to the touch. For Levinas, being *me* consists in being in a relation that he characterizes famously as "face-to-face." It is an encounter with another in which the other is not just an object of perception, consciousness, or cognition, nor is it an adversary in a struggle for dominance, as in Hegel's originary dialectic of master and slave. Being face-to-face with another is precisely the interruption of this dialectic as it is of every form of objectification; it is a relation in which I find myself (prior to any decision on my part) existing for the *good* of the other, responsible for his or her welfare. In Levinas's thinking, I experience myself (for the first time) not as a *cogito* but in the claim that others have on *me*.

What sort of claim might this be? Jean-Paul Sartre in his famous analysis of the *look* treats this as an event of cognition, or more exactly a reversal of cognition in which I become another's representation, part of the furniture of another's consciousness: in other words, a mere object (being looked at, like being brought under a category, is an event of dehumanization).[24] Levinas maps onto this encounter another model—not the Greek or philosophical model of knowing and being known but the Jewish or biblical model of election, the prophetic experience of being summoned out of one's place of comfort and security and placed at the disposal of others. In this situation, I can no longer comport myself as a *cogito*, a subject of reason whether pure or practical, a consciousness conceived in terms of concepts and intentions. Gone likewise are all the basic characters of traditional moral philosophy: the moral spectator, the self-legislating rational actor, the calculator of means and ends, the emotive self, the theorist of the right and the good, the well-formed inhabitant of moral communities. The "ruin of the myth of man," indeed. In the relation of face-to-face, Levinas says, "the word *I* means *here I am* [*me voici*: see me here]," without shelter, no longer in a position of control, answerable to (and for) another (*AE*, 180/*OTB*, 114). The logical subject grasps the world conceptually (that is what the word "concept" means: *Begriff* in German derives from *greifen*, to grasp); being human is the reverse of this: "I am 'in myself' through the others," Levinas says. "The psyche is the other in the same. . . . Backed up against itself, in itself because without any recourse to anything, in itself like in its skin, the self in its skin both is exposed to the exterior (which does not happen to things) and obsessed by the others in this naked exposure" (*AE*, 178/*OTB*, 112). From a Greek standpoint (just to call it that) Levinas's thinking, as he himself put it, "is simply something demented" (*AE*, 178–79/*OTB*, 113):

> Vulnerability, exposure to outrage, to wounding, to passivity more passive than all patience, passivity of the accusative form, trauma of accusation suffered by a hostage to the point of persecution, implicating the identity of the hostage who substitutes himself for others: *all this is the self*, a defecting or defeat of the ego's identity. (*AE*, 31/*OTB*, 15; my emphasis)[25]

Think of the *cogito* turned inside out and reincarnated:

> It is because subjectivity is sensibility—an exposure to others, a vulnerability and a responsibility in the proximity of the others, the one-for-the-other . . . that a subject is of flesh and blood, a man that is hungry and eats, entrails in a skin, and thus capable of giving the bread out of his mouth, or giving his skin. (*AE*, 124/*OTB*, 77)[26]

Not surprisingly, in "Signature" Levinas gives us an autobiography without an "I" or any self-reference: "heteronomy through and through."[27]

Self-Creation

Stanley Cavell has, by contrast, what looks like a straightforwardly Greek approach to this issue: the human is not a natural kind, and in particular *my* humanness, my being anyone, is not a given; it has to be created (we are not beings but creatures). And after the death of God there are only two alternatives, neither of them certain of success: Either I am a cultural product like any other, woven out of the stuff or tissue of material conditions, social relations, ideological systems, family romances, the law of the father, the cultural fabric (what Martin Hollis calls a "plastic man"—"a socially programmed feedback system"); or I am my own creation, self-authored, responsible for my own existence, whatever I am.[28] Cavell affirms "the absolute responsibility of the self to itself," which for him is the main thesis of what he calls "Emersonian perfectionism," where the idea of having a self entails the obligation of self-formation, freeing oneself from the repetitious inertia of social construction.[29] As Cavell says, "the move from the state of nature to the contract of society does not, after all, sufficiently sustain human life" (*CH*, 52). Insofar as I'm simply shaped from the outside-in, I do not exist. Unless I "enact my existence"—that is Cavell's phrase—I merely haunt the world, like a ghost.[30] How to enact one's existence is not self-evident—there is no program, no set of spiritual exercises—but Cavell takes Descartes's *cogito* as an instance of self-authoring, which is what Emerson makes of it in his essay "Self-Reliance," with its idea of self-creation from within a social environment of "bugs" and "spawn."[31] The *cogito* in this respect is not just an argument or an inference; it is an act that we must perform, an originary task, a necessity of existence, but this is not just solitary singing. I do not exist until I am intelligible to others on my own terms (*CH*, 46–47). "Self-Reliance" is nevertheless about how we fall short. Likewise the theme of Thoreau's *Walden* is that none of us is human (or, indeed, anything) yet, that the existence of the human has not yet occurred.[32] The difficulty is: Who would recognize it (and how?) if and when it does occur? In fact, the question of recognition is complex and, indeed, full of uncertainties as to consequences. (We'll see in the next chapter how Cavell, among others, addresses this question.)

For some thinkers, *self*-recognition is what seems to matter. Jean-Paul Sartre's idea, for example, is that in modernity we are all sub- or partially human, shaped from the outside by roles, functions, positions, offices, ranks, rules, types, and ready-to-wear name tags of every kind.[33] Hence the existential double bind. As Sartre says: "I am in the mode of not being what I am and of being what I am not" (*BN*, 365). In this event no one is in a position to say what a human life might be.[34] There is no universal concept or principle in charge here (which is all that the motto "existence precedes essence" means). But—importantly—Sartre takes this absence of any given as a condition of freedom in which the individual, given what is possible in finite situations, faces the task of creating him or herself by way of decision and action: "The doctrine I am putting before you," Sartre says, "is . . . that there is no reality except in action. It goes further and adds, 'Man is nothing else but what he purposes, he exists only insofar as he realizes himself, he is therefore nothing else but the sum of his actions, nothing else but what his life is.'"[35] Being passive with respect to one's existence is just bad faith.

A comparable idea of self-creation is a theme in some of Michel Foucault's later writings, where the point is to reinvent the ancient Greek practice of *epimeleia heautou*, "care of the self," which is a project of self-formation and autonomization through exercises of self-mastery.[36] Foucault emphasizes that his project is not a return to the Greeks; rather, as we learn (says Foucault) from Baudelaire, self-creation is precisely what constitutes modernity: "Modern man, for Baudelaire, is not the man who goes off to discover himself, his secrets and his hidden truth; he is the man who tries to invent himself. This modernity does not 'liberate man in his own being'; it compels him to face the task of producing himself."[37] Asked how his "aesthetics of the self" differs from Sartrean existentialism, Foucault replied: "I think that the only acceptable practical consequence of what Sartre has said is to link his theoretical insight [that the self is not something given to us] to the practice of creativity—and not that of authenticity. From the idea that the self is not given to us, I think that there is only one practical consequence: we have to create ourselves as a work of art" (*E*, 262). To which Foucault added that his position is closer to Nietzsche's (*The Gay Science*, §290) than to Sartre's. But it is also a more complex and open-ended position, as we'll see in Chapter 3 below, because it entails (at the very least) a critical self-relation that one misses, for example, in Richard Rorty's "liberal irony," which is an up-to-date version of the romantic idea of "living poetically," composing oneself ex nihilo, as well as of Nietzsche's idea of "self-knowledge as self-creation," where "to fail as a *human* being . . . is to accept somebody else's description of oneself, to execute a previously prepared program."[38] And if we ask, what comes out in the end? the answer is: at the level of particularity in which all that matters is *oneself*, anything goes. Hence the thick line that Rorty draws between private and public selves. Basically we can only self-create in the dark. It is a process (Rorty thinks, as did Sartre) in which others tend to interfere.[39]

Without Identity

However, the matter is complicated if one follows the argument that at ground level my relationship to myself is apt to be (how shall we say?) *circumspect*, that is, not a relation of observation or reflection—nothing so clear and distinct as a *cogito*—but, as Manfred Frank puts it, simply a tacit experience of being on familiar terms with myself. Theoretical categories of "subject" and "object" are inadequate to this familiarity, and so is the term "knowledge." There is only *me*, Frank says, "whoever I am."

> I may be a brain swimming desolately in the vat of the experimentation of a sadistic neurobiologist (and whose nerve endings are connected to a supercomputer). Even when I know nothing more at all about my bodily appearance (because I have never seen myself in that circumstance, nor will I ever get to see me or in any other way perceive me)—even then, I can always grasp the thought, "My God, I won't let this happen again." And the "I" in these thoughts refers with dead certainty to *me*, even when I have no perception and no description of myself. It is otherwise with the objective use of "I." This occurs in propositions such as "I have a bump on my forehead" or "I am standing next to the table." In both cases "I" refers not to the logical subject of the thought but rather to my body (or a part of it or to its location, etc.)—but *that* this is so, I need not know. I need not feel the bump, and I may not have seen the table. I obtain this information only by perception. And in the case of direct epistemological self-reference there is nothing that I can fail to perceive or in whose identification I could go astray. "I" is just not an object of perception that I could identify as the self that has the perception.[40]

In other words, familiarity with myself does not reach the level of self-knowledge or self-identity, much less self-representation; it is rather a finite form of acceptance, no doubt in equal parts recognition and resignation: this (something) is now happening to *me*, and so as time goes by, with all that happens, I grow accustomed to being *me*. Whether anything so substantive as a self, much less a *human* self, not to mention an "aesthetics of the self," can be formed from this tacit state of affairs is an open question: being *me* may not all by itself be a ground or basis on which any edification could rely. After all, "who is *me*?" (and can it be made the subject or object of any predicate?). Who is me? Levinas would answer: "no one." In an essay on "Bad Conscience and the Inexorable," Levinas emphasizes the indirect or tacit nature of one's awareness of oneself. On the one hand, consciousness as such is intentional, directed toward the world; on the other, as Husserl pointed out long ago, there is also consciousness of mental activity—but this (so-called) reflexive consciousness is, Levinas says, "without intentional aim," nor can it be made the object of "the scrutinizing and thematizing and objectivizing and indiscreet eye of reflection":

> As a dim consciousness, an implicit consciousness preceding all intentions— or coming back from all intentions—it is not an act, but rather a pure passivity. . . . It is a "consciousness" that, rather than signifying self-knowledge, is effacement or discretion of presence. A bad conscience [*mauvaise conscience*: one could perhaps paraphrase, "poor consciousness"]: without intentions, without aims, under the protective mask of the personage contemplating himself in the mirror of the world, assured and positing himself. *This consciousness is without a name, without situation, without titles. A presence that dreads presence, naked of all attributes.* Its nudity is not that of disclosure or exposure to view of the truth. In its non-intentionality, prior to all willing and before all fault, in its non-intentional identification, identity recoils before its affirmation. . . . The interiority of mental life is, perhaps, originally this. (my emphasis)[41]

Who is *me*? Levinas answers: "It is first a non-quiddity, no one [*personne*], clothed with purely borrowed being, which masks its nameless singularity by conferring on it a role" (*AE*, 168/*OTB*, 106). Being oneself (*soi-même*) eludes one's own grasp, as if one were a kind of Eurydice. "The oneself comes from a past that could not be remembered, not because it is situated very far behind, but because the oneself, incommensurable with consciousness which is always equal to itself, is not 'made' for the present. . . . It is the identity of the singular, modified only in the erosion of ageing, in the permanent loss of self. It is unsayable and thus unjustifiable" (*AE*, 169/*OTB*, 107). This is not, Levinas is quick to add, any kind of anthropocentric version of negative theology: "These negative qualifications of the subjectivity of oneself do not consecrate some ineffable mystery, but confirm the presynthetic, prelogical and in a certain sense atomic, that is, in-dividual unity of the self, which prevents it from splitting, separating itself from itself so as to contemplate or express itself, and thus show itself, if only under a comic mask, to name itself otherwise than by a pro-noun" (*AE*, 169/*OTB*, 107). It is rather that I am a subjectivity without a subject—until I become subject to another's claim, redeemed (so to speak) by the accusative voice that summons me out of my clandestine self to exist for another. I am not I (whoever I may be) until another interrogates me.[42]

Sovereignty

But what if there were no Other? (A question no Levinasian has yet imagined.)

A text that addresses just this question in beautifully complex ways is Michel Tournier's novel *Vendredi, ou les limbes du Pacifique* (*Friday*), a rewriting (or reinvention) of Daniel Defoe's *The Strange and Surprising Adventures of Robinson Crusoe*. Defoe's novel, whatever else it is, is a master-narrative of bourgeois autonomy and self-sufficiency. Reduced to himself, deprived of a human world, Defoe's Crusoe certainly suffers his afflictions—fear, remorse, guilt, illness, loneliness, despair; but these afflictions do not affect his self-possession. His experience of himself and his predicament is painful, but it is not an experience of self-estrangement; on the contrary, his construction of a human economy from degree zero (his "civilizing" of the island) is a parable of self-justification, an assertion of rational autonomy.

In Tournier's version everything is conceived differently. In the absence of others, Tournier's Crusoe undergoes (initially, and almost without noticing it) a transformation into something analogous to Giorgio Agamben's conception "bare life" (*zoē*), a condition of exteriority in which, by a sovereign decision (or occasion) of abandonment or banishment, a human being ceases to be regarded, experienced, or treated as human (may, for example, be killed with impunity).[43] Bare life is, so to speak, without predicates.

Interestingly, the first indication of Crusoe's metamorphosis occurs in his encounter with an animal:

> Looking around, he met the gaze of Tenn, the *Virginia*'s dog, a setter of doubtful breeding but warmly affectionate disposition. It had stopped a few yards away and was observing him with ears cocked and one forepaw raised. A great happiness flooded through Robinson. After all, he was not the only survivor of the wreck! He walked toward the animal, speaking its name. Tenn was one of those dogs who have an absolute need of human companionship, the sound of a human voice, and the touch of a human hand. It was strange, then, that instead of running to greet Robinson with his tail wagging he should have backed away, furiously growling, with teeth bared. He turned abruptly and bolted into the wood. (*V*, 32/*F*, 34)

Crusoe imagines that, in its castoff state, the dog has simply undergone a regression: "Perhaps they had been so long on the island that the dog had simply reverted to its natural, wild state. How long was it since the shipwreck? How many days, weeks, months, even years had passed. He was assailed with a kind of dizziness when he asked the question" (*V*, 32/*F*, 35)—for, indeed, Crusoe exists now in a condition in which the passing of time, and hence change itself, no longer registers as a fact of experience. But in fact it is Tenn, the dog, who is unchanged: being "one of those dogs who have an absolute need for human companionship, the sound of a human voice, the touch of a human hand," Tenn reacts as if Crusoe were no longer a human being. Only there is no *as if*. Tenn is simply bearing witness to what Crusoe has yet to discover, namely that *l'absence d'autrui* is a *force of dehumanization*, and that Crusoe is ceasing to be human. The question the novel raises is whether this cessation is an altogether bad thing.

A critical turning point is Crusoe's failed effort to build a vessel that would enable him to escape the island (which he initially names *Desolation*); or, more exactly (since he does in fact construct such a thing, which he christens, appropriately, *Escape*), what is crucial is his failure to foresee that the vessel (a hollowed-out tree trunk) is just too large and heavy to transport to the water's edge. Pointedly, the failure does not surprise Crusoe; its possibility just never had occurred to him—because the absence of others and their perspectives has eliminated "the category of the possible" from his horizon of experience.[44] However construed, the failure of foresight proves critical: in despair Crusoe abandons himself to "bare life," becoming a creature that makes its home in a swamp:

> Then a human form, like a statue of clay, rose and made its way through the reeds [*C'est alors qu'une statue de limon s'anima à son tour et glissa au milieu des joncs*; the translation *rehumanizes* Crusoe]. Robinson could not have said how long it was since he had left his last shred of clothing on some thornbush. In any case, the thought of sunburn no longer troubled him, since his back, flanks, and thighs were now protected by a thick coating of dried mud. His hair and beard had grown so long that his face was almost invisible beneath their tangled mass. His hands had become mere forepaws used for walking, since it made him giddy to stand upright. His state of physical weakness and the softness of sand and mud, but above all the breaking of some little spring within his soul, had led him to move only on his hands and knees. He knew now that man resembles a person injured in a street riot, who can only stay upright while the crowd packed densely around him continues to prop him up. Exiled from the mass of his fellows, who sustained him as a part of humanity without his realizing it, he felt that he no longer had the strength to stand on his own feet. He lived on unmentionable foods, gnawing them with his face to the ground. He relieved himself where he lay, and rarely failed to roll in the damp warmth of his own excrement. He moved less and less, and his brief excursions always ended in his return to the mire. (*V*, 38/*F*, 40)

Interestingly, in this state of "bare life" all that remains of Crusoe the man is his memory, and it is *this* (in the form of a hallucination in which Crusoe comes face-to-face with his sister, long since dead) that saves him, or at any rate leads him to realize that "only a little more was needed to degrade him utterly and to drive him to the depths of madness. Under pain of death he must find the strength to tear himself away from it. . . . He must once again take his life in hand" (*V*, 42/*F*, 44).

At which point *Vendredi* becomes (almost) a novel of self-creation, not so much because Crusoe (as he does in Defoe's version) recivilizes himself in the bargain of civilizing the island—taking things, including himself, in hand turns out to be a failed and, indeed, blasted project—as because the island that he tries to tame (rechristened, in a utopian moment, *Speranza*) turns him into something autochthonous: his intimacy with the island is an achievement of a form of life free of the human order of things—and therefore, in the nature of the case, a bit difficult to describe since it cannot "be translated into human language [*en termes humains*]" (*V*, 230/*F*, 212).

Crusoe's apotheosis is made possible by the arrival of Friday, because Friday is himself outside the human order. As if full-blown from the brow of Rousseau, he is an unspoiled creature of natural self-sufficiency who seems incapable of any form of alienation (too bad that, as the novel intimates, he will in the end in all likelihood be sold into slavery). It is Friday who initiates Crusoe into a temporality in which time ceases to pass. By accident, Friday sets off a cache of explosives that obliterates much of what Crusoe has constructed on Esperanza, the result of which is to liberate from Crusoe from his work and from the time of work, that is, from his past but also from any attention to the future or the time of possibility. As Crusoe expresses it in his journal: *"Formerly every day, hour, and minute leaned in a sense toward the day, hour, and minute that was to follow. . . . So time passed rapidly and usefully, the more quickly because it was usefully employed, leaving behind it an accumulation of achievement and wastage which was part of my history"* (*V*, 218/*F*, 203). The new temporality is the circular time of the sun in which Crusoe becomes ageless—"younger today than the pious and self-seeking young man who had set sail in the *Virginia*, not young with a biological youth, but with a mineral youth, solar and divine. Every day was for him a first beginning, an absolute beginning of the history of the world. Beneath the rays of the sun-god, Speranza trembled in an eternal present, without past or future. He could not forsake that eternal instant, poised at the needle point of ecstasy, to sink back into a world of usury, dust, and decay" (*V*, 246/*F*, 226). Crusoe is only himself (who- or whatever that is) from the moment the sun rises until it sets; otherwise, as when others appear, he is in danger of regression.

The danger arrives in the form of a ship, the *Whitebird* from Blackpool, whose captain and crew come ashore to replenish their food and water supply, which they do by literally plundering the island, making off with its fruit, vegetables, and goats. Rescue at last? At the appearance of the boat full of sailors Crusoe "had a vision, like that of a drowning man, of his whole life on the island—the building of the *Escape*, the mire, the frenetic cultivation of Speranza . . . the coming of Friday, the explosion—above all, the measureless extent of time during which his conversion to the sun had been completed in tranquil happiness" (*V*, 234/*F*, 216). Could he transport this solar form of life back to civilization? (Does he want to?) He regards the sailors and the captain (and, indeed, himself as one of them) with a kind of anthropological detachment or disinterest, realizing "that in former times he had been as they were, driven by the same motives of greed, arrogance, and violence, and that a part of him was still one with them" (*V*, 238/*F*, 220). However, watching Friday's happy embrace of the ship, with its riggings and crosstrees that serve him as a kind of playground, Crusoe becomes "conscious of his own growing revulsion for this world [of the ship], into which he was being dragged, it seemed to him, against his will" (*V*, 242/*F*, 223)—a revulsion that increases when he encounters the unfortunate Jaan, the abused galley boy who constitutes the lowest form of life aboard ship (and so within the human order of things). As sunset arrives, he decides to remain on the island (meanwhile Friday chooses civilization; Jaan—with his red hair, the image of Robinson as a boy—deserts the ship to join Crusoe in his solitude).

What is the meaning of this decision to remain? (Who, or what, has Crusoe become?) In *The Inhuman*, Lyotard asks: "What shall we call human in humans, the initial misery of their childhood, or their capacity to acquire a 'second' nature which, thanks to language, makes them fit to share in communal life, adult consciousness, and reason? That the second presupposes the first is agreed by everyone. The question is only that of knowing whether this dialectic, whatever name we grace it with, leaves no remainder" (*I*, 3). Rousseau-like, Lyotard thinks that the child is "eminently the human," and that in the "civilizing process" we cease being human in the bargain of becoming productive citizens. "All education is inhuman," says Lyotard (*I*, 4–5). Hence Friday's absolute and carefree sovereignty.

On this line of thinking, what Tournier's Crusoe achieves is something like freedom from the "civilizing process" of which he was once the perfect embodiment when he extracted from Speranza a productive economy, producing for all the world a bourgeois order of domination and exchange. This freedom seems to be the conceptual point of the "solar experience" that rescues Crusoe from time and the idea that time must be put to use in behalf of the future. Here it becomes possible to read *Vendredi* as an allegory of Georges Bataille's conception of sovereignty. As Bataille says, "Life beyond utility is the domain of sovereignty."[45] Sovereignty is not Lockean or Kantian but anarchic—a condition of exteriority:

> To know is always to strive, to work: it is always a servile operation, indefinitely resumed, indefinitely repeated. Knowledge is never sovereignty: to be *sovereign* it would have to occur in a moment. But the moment remains outside, short of or beyond, all knowledge. We know regular sequences in time, constants; we know nothing, absolutely, of what is not in the image of an operation, a servile modality of being, subordinate to the future, to its concatenation in time. We know nothing absolutely, of the moment. (*AS*, 202)

Crusoe's solar experience is an experience of this moment of sovereignty outside time and the future—"the miraculous moment . . . when *anticipation dissolves into* NOTHING" (*AS*, 207). It is an experience of the sacred—or, alternatively, it is an experience that transforms Crusoe into something sacred, something (in Bataille's words) outside "the subordination that characterizes the world": "the world of things or of practice . . . in which man is subjugated, or simply in which he serves some purpose, whether or not he is servant to another. Man is alienated therein, he is himself a thing." By contrast, "the sovereign man . . . alone enjoys a nonalienated condition. He alone has a condition comparable to that of the wild animal, and he is sacred, being above things" (*AS*, 214).

Sovereign Man: someone free of identity—someone no one nor any system can track down or confine: and so perhaps no longer human, neither human nor nonhuman but a figure of alterity without reference to the same.⁴⁶ The interesting question is: What sort of relation could we have with such a creature? Tournier's answer seems to lie in the young outcast, Jaan, who recognizes in Crusoe an alternative form of life, or at all events someone to be with—*Mitsein*: a condition not available to Jaan in the human world that regards him as a thing. Recall Lyotard on "the initial misery of childhood." Jaan is perhaps now free, as is Crusoe, to be inhuman: than which there is perhaps no better (or anyhow freer) form of life.

What Is Human Recognition?

(ON ZONES OF INDISTINCTION)

"I am I because my little dog knows me"
Let me begin with Ovid's story of Actaeon from *The Metamorphoses*. You will remember that he is the hunter who stumbles upon the goddess Diana as she is bathing in a stream. Outraged at being seen, or looked at, she transforms him into a deer:

> She uttered no more threats, but made horns of a long-lived stag sprout where she had scattered water on his brow. She lengthened his neck, brought the tips of his ears to a point, changed his hands to feet, his arms to long legs, and covered his body with a dappled skin. Then she put panic fear into his heart as well. The hero fled, and even as he ran, marveled to find himself so swift. When he glimpsed his face and his horns, reflected in the water, he tried to say "Alas!" but no words came. He groaned—that was all the voice he had—and tears ran down his changed cheeks. Only his mind remained the same as before.[1]

At this point he is spotted by his dogs, each one of which Ovid pauses to name. Actaeon flees, longing to cry out, "'I am Actaeon! Don't you know your own master?'" But his words don't form; Actaeon can only groan, "uttering such a sound which, though not human, was yet such as no stag could produce. The ridges he knew so well were filled with his mournful cries. Falling to his knees, like a suppliant in prayer, he silently swayed his head this way and that, as if stretched out beseeching arms. His friends, not knowing what they did, urged on the ravening mob with their usual encouragements and looked around for Actaeon, shouted for Actaeon, as if he were not there, each trying to call louder than the other. . . . Actaeon turned his head at the sound of his name. Well might he wish to be absent, but he was all too surely present" (80).

There are some curious things in this narrative. The first is that, in ceasing to be human, Actaeon does not quite cease being human; that is, ceasing is in some sense interminable. It is as if Actaeon had entered into a temporality somewhat different from the logical or familiar order of things (think of it as the temporality of suffering or of dying—the temporality of flesh).[2] At all events he is turned objectively or, let us say, biologically into a stag, but subjectively he remains who he is, or rather "his mind remained the same as before," but he no longer answers, or can answer, to the name "Actaeon." Or perhaps subjectivity is what he loses in the sense that it can no longer be ascribed to him by others. What we have in the story is something like what Stanley Cavell calls the myth (or horror) of *inexpressiveness* ("of the mind unmoored, say unhinged, leaving itself without material in which to realize and communicate itself" [CR, 472]). Ceasing to be human means losing one's voice, that is, losing one's capacity for being recognized as human: imagine belonging to an order of things absolutely unresponsive to your existence. Of course Ovid's story is about the failure of recognition, or of reidentification, but one wonders, what would the story have been like had Actaeon's friends been able to recognize him, changes and all? What would *their* experience have been like? How respond to someone who is no longer (visibly) human but not, or not yet, wholly otherwise? Actaeon is an anomalous creature of the between: neither human nor nonhuman but inhuman (or *ahuman*), that is, monstrous. Monstrous, yet in some ways not. The story belongs to the genre of the hunter hunted. The most distinctive feature of Actaeon as a hunter is his gentleness and restraint. His metamorphosis thus expresses a certain side of him; he isn't turned into something completely alien, rather something alien in him—something out of character or out of keeping with his friends and his dogs, not to say his profession—is, so to speak, brought out and exposed to others. Had he been turned into a wolf his dogs might have had a more exacting time of it, but he was never wolf-like in the manner of Lycaon, whom Jupiter transformed into a wolf as punishment for his incorrigible bloodthirsty habits.

Interestingly, "lycanthropy" is still occasionally used as the name of a psychiatric disorder in which one ceases to experience oneself as a human being. There is even a book called *The Lycanthropy Reader*, on the prevalence of werewolves in human history: werewolves—and monsters generally—are, it appears, the natural companions of human beings, indispensable to attempts, futile as they may be, at human self-understanding.[3] In a book called *Monster Theory* Jeffrey Cohen remarks that monsters have always been basic to the fragile equilibrium of human self-definition, and are apt to dominate a culture's most popular images during periods of social and political instability and crisis (there are probably no other sorts of period in human history).[4]

Just so, historically the werewolf—*wargus*—is simply someone who ceases to be human by being banished from the community; he becomes, in Giorgio Agamben's expression, a *homo sacer*, sacred in the sense of set apart or accursed. Agamben writes:

> What had to remain in the collective unconscious as a monstrous hybrid of human and animal, divided between the forest and the city—the werewolf—is, therefore, in its origin the figure of the man who has been banned from the city. That such a man is defined as a wolf-man and not simply as a wolf (the expression *caput lupinum* has the form of a juridical statute) is decisive here. The life of the bandit, like that of sacred man, is not a piece of animal nature without any relation to law and the city. It is, rather, a threshold of indistinction and a passage between animal and man, *physis* and *nomos*, exclusion and inclusion: the life of the bandit is the life of the *loup garou*, the werewolf, who is precisely *neither man nor beast*, and who dwells paradoxically within both without belonging to either. (HS, 105)

As if my being human (or not) were dependent, not on knowledge of one kind or another, or on some fact, but on a decision or judgment—a bestowal or refusal of recognition—one determined perhaps by some act or conduct forbidden to human beings (fratricide, incest, banditry, bestiality), but of course anything might count as a taboo, since taboos are always local and contingent (in which case, so would be the condition of being human). What is interesting about the werewolf is that, outcast though he is (if "he" is the word), he remains internal to the order that banished him as the limit-concept of its anthropology. He marks the "threshold of indistinction and passage between animal and man" to which human beings and animals are always exposed.

Porous Subjects

There are clearly many zones of indistinction both ancient and modern. Consider, for example, the anthropology implicit in Ovid's text. It pictures the human being as porous and exposed, liable at any moment to be rinsed like a washcloth by whatever surrounds it. It is an anthropology that can properly be called demonic, where the boundaries that pick out the human from the divine on the one hand and from the animal on the other are highly unstable, with a good deal of traffic moving back and forth in every direction. This is perhaps a Hellenic rather than Jewish anthropology. There are (to be strict about it) mortals but no humans in Greek antiquity, where heroes regularly show divine ancestry and, in their finest moments, behave like lions. Arguably, being human might just be a biblical concept. I mean that, perhaps owing to the absolute alterity of God, the human is more sharply delineated, has firmer boundaries, in the Hebrew Bible than in ancient Greek culture, at least until the time of Aristotle (even Socrates has his daimon). In the Scriptures people are turned into salt but not into animals or other sorts of creatures, and of course the idea of turning into God cannot be thought. If people turn to stone, it is because their hearts have hardened.[5] By contrast, Ovid's is a non-egocentric anthropology without much interior/exterior structure. The human being is not sealed off from whatever is not itself but is open to invasion from the other (from *Eros* or *Eris*), the eyes being particularly vulnerable in this respect. The "I"—let's call it, out of courtesy to philosophical tradition, the logical subject, the disengaged punctual ego exercising or trying for self-possession and rational control—the "I" is always in danger of being lost or overtaken and must struggle to preserve its integrity. Much of Western literature seems to be about this struggle in which failure is frequent and always gripping.

The literary genre in which this anthropology and this struggle are most fully explored seems to be that of tragedy (with the Gothic novel no doubt a close second), in which the human is defined by its condition of exposure or vulnerability to savagery and madness, as if the existence of the human could only be registered in the moment of its disappearance. In ancient tragedy savagery and madness are frequently represented by women absorbed in ferocious acts of murder and dismemberment, most famously perhaps as Maenads in *The Bacchae* of Euripides. In tragedy the "I" or sovereign logical subject is exposed to the feminine; in this event it is no longer an "I" but a "me," that is, no longer a subject *of* but now a subject *to* experience, all of it bad. Crossing the threshold that separates the public world of action and discourse from the household, the *polis* from the *oikos*, men from women, is a movement from "I" to "me," from one who acts to one who is exposed, from the assertive to the receptive and the passivity of suffering. It is a movement into a different temporality from that of human action. It is a movement in which being human always enters a condition of crisis of recognition—in *The Bacchae* Dionysus, appearing as a beautiful, androgynous youth, persuades Pentheus, king of Thebes, to disguise himself as a woman in order to observe unobserved the Maenads in their frenzy. But as frequently happens in literature, the disguise invades and transforms the subjectivity of the disguised: the mask is magical. Pentheus grows effeminate and weak, and in this defenseless feminine state he is torn to pieces by his mother, Agauë, who in her madness imagines that she is dismembering a bull. The recognition scene consists of Agauë regaining her senses and discovering that she is holding as her trophy the disembodied head of her son. I like to think of this as the purest moment of tragedy in all of Greek tragedy.[6] It is somewhat easier for male readers to contemplate Oedipus, who has no trouble giving the correct answer to the riddle of the Sphinx, but whose shame on learning his true identity makes even the everyday experience of human recognition intolerable. And so Oedipus puts out his eyes, which a Nietzschean might read as an escape from the limits or confinement of the human, that is, as a movement of self-transcendence; in any case, he becomes a kind of *homo sacer*, haunting the borders of cities.

The Vanishing of the Human

Many years ago the critic Northrop Frye introduced a picture of literary or cultural history that seems worth preserving: namely, that Western culture "has steadily moved its center of gravity" from a mythic or heroic anthropology to one that is ironic, where a threshold waits to be crossed into the no longer human.[7] Robert Musil located this threshold in a scathing satire, *The Man Without Qualities*—notice again the metaphor of the porous subject:

> For the inhabitant of [any] country has at least nine characters: a professional one, a national one, a civic one, a class one, a geographical one, a sex one, a conscious one, an unconscious and perhaps even too a private one; he combines them all in himself, but they dissolve him, and he is really nothing but a little channel washed out by all these trickling streams, which flow into it and drain out of it again in order to join other little streams filling another little channel.[8]

The irony here registers a judgment like Max Weber's familiar idea that modern bourgeois culture—or modernity, for short—is, whatever else it is, a powerful mechanism of disenchantment, that is, a rationalized system for draining away human subjectivity, leaving behind a social torpor of "routinized habitual blind ethical obedience and passivity."[9] These words belong to a political theorist who made a list of Weber's metaphors of modernity: "Petrification, darkness, mechanization—emptiness, inner death; no spirit, no vision. Routine, non-creative energy; a world of shadows without true substance. An iron cage. Prisoners of a denatured culture, subjects of massive, bureaucratized institutions, victims of the ferocity and impersonality of capitalist market economy; prisoners oblivious to the meaning of freedom. Exiles unable to recall visions of the promised land. Modern urban life: totally detached from Nature, insular, dispirited, lonely" (231). With less hyperbole, Stanley Cavell in *The Claim of Reason* refers to this condition as "the vanishing of the human," and he thinks of it as a futurist fantasy in which one day the experience, or fact, of ceasing to be human would no longer fill people with alarm, or even with dissatisfaction, because nothing would any longer give them "the idea that living things, human beings, could feel. So they would not (any longer) be human. They would not, for example, be frightened upon meeting [other human beings]—except . . . under circumstances in which they would be frightened upon encountering bears or storms, circumstances in which bears would be frightened. And of course particular forms of laughter and amazement would also no longer be possible, ones which depend upon clear breaks between, say, machines and creatures" (*CR*, 468).

Naturally one thinks of Kafka's great story "The Metamorphosis," in which Gregor Samsa awakens after a night of "unquiet dreams" to find himself transformed into a bug. It is interesting to know that, except for Arachne, no one in Ovid's *Metamorphoses* is turned into an insect (and a spider, strictly speaking, is not an insect). A major irony of Kafka's story is that Gregor's transformation is merely a case of biology struggling to keep pace with social evolution and the hypertrophy of an administered world. But what is most unsettling, given Cavell's perspective, is that Gregor is not horrified by what has happened to him. Recall that upon discovering that he is now a bug Gregor's first thought is of going back to sleep, and his second is that now he will surely be late for work and "be sacked on the spot" (*KCS*, 90). Gregor's parents and sister remember him as someone who liked nothing so much as reading train schedules, which he did almost every evening until bedtime. Max Weber would say that our culture had done a superb job in preparing Gregor psychologically for his transformation (although—importantly—Deleuze and Guattari see the change as a "line of escape" from the regimes of office and family).[10] In any case, Gregor, like Actaeon, retains his first-person perspective—being a *me* who worries, as no one else can, about *me*—even though he has ceased to be recognizable (is no longer an "I"): his speech, after all, is now only "an unbearable hissing noise" (*KCS*, 104) that makes people chase him with a stick. The reason he keeps hold of his inwardness is that, appearances aside, his family continues to treat him as (something like) Gregor, occupying (at least) Gregor's place. His sister feeds him, for example, and of course he is allowed to stay in his room; he responds by crawling under his bed at feeding time in order to spare his family the sight of his repulsiveness.

But then suddenly things change. The crucial moment occurs when Gregor's mother and sister formally withdraw their recognition of him as Gregor by removing his furniture from his room. Here, if anywhere, is where Gregor is taken across the fatal threshold that defines the existence of the human: "They were clearing his room out; taking away everything he loved; the chest in which he kept his fret saw and other tools was already dragged off; they were now loosening the writing desk which had almost sunk to the floor, the desk at which he had done all his homework when he was at the commercial academy, at the grammar school before that, and, yes, even at the primary school" (*KCS*, 118). As if, in strict moral accord with the bourgeois order of things, Gregor's identity, his inwardness, his being human, were *in* his furniture.[11] So much for the first-person perspective, which is perhaps capable of floating freely outside the subject, or folding inside out.[12]

Recall that Jacques Lacan, in an essay on "The Freudian Thing," asks, "Is the difference between the desk and us, as far as consciousness is concerned, so very great?" After all, a richer story of human life can be got from a desk, with its accumulation of letters, receipts, overdue bills, and yellowed photographs, than by interrogating the interior of the psyche, supposing there to be such a place.[13] Wittgenstein meanwhile imagines a "chair thinking to itself"—but where, exactly, does its thinking occur?

> WHERE? In one of its parts? Or outside its body; in the air around it? Or not *anywhere* at all? But then what is the difference between this chair's saying something to itself and another one's doing so, next to it? —But then how is it with man: where does *he* say things to himself? How does it come about that this question seems senseless; and that no specification of a place is necessary except just that this man is saying something to himself? Whereas the question *where* the chair talks to itself seems to demand an answer. —The reason is: we want to know *how* the chair is supposed to be like a human being; whether, for instance, the head is at the top of the back and so on." (*Philosophical Investigations* §361)

We could say that Kafka re-enchants the world by causing people in it to cease being human, but only *almost* or *not quite*. To put it perhaps more simply, the characters in his world inhabit an open border where humans and animals (or even things, like Odradek) are interchangeable. In "The Burrow," a burrowing creature of some indeterminate kind constructs an underground home for itself (again according to meticulous bourgeois protocol), but the possession of the house, that is, the experience of possession itself, or perhaps one should say the attempt at self-possession, produces so deep an insecurity in the animal that it cannot rest, cannot keep still, but in fact has to maintain an endless vigil outside its entrance against possible invasion from an imaginary "great beast" (*KCS*, 353). In fact an invasion occurs, but in the form of a mysterious incessant humming sound that cannot be closed out (noise as a parasite). It is as if Kafka were resurrecting the ancient anthropology of the porous mortal. As the sound cannot be kept out, so neither can the mind be kept in: it drains away in an interminable paranoia. Of course, the beast is, in every respect, already within—and it would not be difficult to show that this is a basic and persistent trope of modern anthropology: the inhuman is internal to the human as part of its deep biological, psychological, and even moral structure, and what we call civilization consists in the mechanisms of repression and sublimation or, alternatively, of social evolution and cultural formation, that make it possible for us to inhabit human society. The human Id is not, so to speak, human. As if we were porous not with respect to the external powers of gods and demons but inwardly with respect to our alien or at all events plural selves ("The alien being must be in me," Kafka writes in his *Diaries* [58]). Human beings are, let us say, hosts of the inhuman.[14] The human is not made of anything human (the moral, in a way, of Mary Shelley's *Frankenstein*, not to mention Daniel Dennett's "anti-homuncularism").[15] Every Jekyll has his Hyde. Anyway, the question is, How keep others out of the first person, or out of one's self-relation? Perhaps this is modernity's version of the old Greek or tragic dilemma.

Kafka's "Report to the Academy" is a wonderful parody of modernity's dilemma, a kind of upside-down behaviorist allegory of civilization and its discontents. The report is an ape's address to a scientific gathering in which he explains how he ceased to be (merely) an ape. An expedition to Africa took him captive, and during his confinement in a makeshift cage on board the ship that transported him to Europe it came to him (he can't recall how) that the only way out of his predicament was "to stop being an ape" (*KCS*, 253), that is, to imitate the behavior of humans, which he does without the least trouble by mimicking the antics of the simian sailors who gather around his cage each night to amuse themselves by teaching him to spit and smoke and drink and rub his belly; in other words, he learns how to perform, as if the human were simply a social practice, a performative product. The critical moment occurs when the ape gets drunk one evening and accidentally shouts "Hallo!" With this outburst, he says, "I broke into the human community" (*KCS*, 257). We must understand that this is not a moral achievement but simply a strategy of survival, as is the ape's first crucial decision: "When I was handed over to my first trainer in Hamburg I soon realized that there were two alternatives before me: the Zoological Gardens or the variety stage. I did not hesitate. I said to myself: do your utmost to get onto the variety stage; the Zoological Gardens means only a new cage; once there, you are done for" (*KCS*, 257–58). And so, with the help of tutors (one of whom goes mad and has to be confined), he enlarges his repertoire—"one learns when one has to; one learns when one needs a way out; one learns at all costs. One stands over oneself with a whip; one flays oneself at the slightest opposition. My ape nature fled out of me, head over heels and away.... With an effort which up till now has never been repeated I managed to reach the cultural level of an average European. In itself that might be nothing to speak of, but it is something insofar as it has helped me out of my cage and opened a special way out for me, the way of humanity" (*KCS*, 258). He becomes a celebrated and wealthy entertainer—with a proper name, "Red Peter"—and now enjoys fine wine, admiring visitors, sophisticated conversation (good breeding, as they say). Moreover, he now keeps a pet or, more accurately (European that he has become), a mistress—"a half-trained chimpanzee." "I take comfort from her as apes do. By day I cannot bear to see her; for she has the insane look of the bewildered half-broken animal in her eye; no one else sees it, but I do, and I cannot bear it" (*KCS*, 259).[16]

On Being Monstrous

Naturally one has to ask: What can he not bear to see in the eyes of his mistress? One might suppose it is his own monstrous condition, which is that of someone who has become (by sheer force of will?) human, but who still resides in an animal body. One could do worse than take recourse again to Agamben's conception of "bare life," that is, life as it is lived on the other (perhaps hither) side of being human: a border that, unfortunately, is not fixed or settled in itself but can only be located by a decision or judgment, namely whether or not to grant something of oneself to the other that would extend the border a little further—open it—in the other's behalf. In Kafka's story, human beings seem to have accepted the ape as, more or less, one of them, a fact which may reflect either favorably or poorly on us depending on who we are. But what would it mean for the ape to respond (and not just react) to the look in his mistress's eye? What does it means to respond?

In the final section of *The Claim of Reason*, "Between Acknowledgment and Avoidance," Stanley Cavell writes: "Being human is the power to grant being human. Something about flesh and blood elicits this grant from us, and something about flesh and blood repels it" (*CR*, 397). For Cavell, there are upper and lower limits to being human but nothing like an idea that could "be captured in a definition which specifies a genus" (*CR*, 398). With respect to the first (the upper limit): as a thought experiment Cavell imagines a craftsman who constructs an automaton (referred to as "our friend") that to all appearances looks and moves like a human being (he can light up and enjoy a cigarette, for example) but in fact when opened up for inspection is shown to be a machine, all wires, gears, and pulleys; but the craftsman tinkers away, producing improvements. One day he calls me in to look at his latest version:

> He insists that I pay special attention to each of our procedures. The legs and the hands are now really astonishing. The movement of the legs crossing and of the cigarette being lit are simply amazing. I want to see it all again. And as for the voice, I would bet anything that no one could tell. So far I'm dazzled. Then the craftsman knocks off the hat to reveal what is for all the world a human head, intact. He rotates it through about 45 degrees and then

stops himself with an embarrassed smile. The head turns back to its original position, but now its eyes turn toward mine. Then the knife is produced. As it approaches the friend's side, he suddenly leaps up, as if threatened, and starts grappling with the craftsman. They both grunt, and they are yelling. The friend is producing these words: "No more. It hurts. It hurts too much. I'm sick of being a human guinea pig. I mean a guinea pig human." (CR, 405)

Cavell's question is: "Do I intervene?" What is my responsibility toward an automaton who can nevertheless experience the fear of pain—or, for all we know, can experience pain itself? That is, real pain. But what is that? How to tell real from artificial pain? The line between real and artificial (where parts leave off and mere flesh begins) may be irrelevant: the situation calls for a moral decision on my part, not for further inspection of the automaton, who may be said to have crossed a border into "my" form of life. A question that one derives from Cavell is: What if there were (in principle) no one or nothing to which this border is closed? What if I were the border guard with no settled criteria as to who or what may be allowed to enter?

As if the upper limit of being human were an open border that we nevertheless close for no good reason, or as if to protect a fragile self-importance. Recall Montaigne's famous complaint, in the *Apology for Raymond Sebond*, that human beings are niggardly when it comes to acknowledging the gifts and virtues of other creatures; we human beings refuse to see that animals are not deficient in relation to ourselves, rather it is the other way around: we are deficient with respect to others. The assumption that animals are incapable of speech is simply a consequence of our inability to understand them—the way we are helpless to understand the intricate singing of whales. Hassan Melehy writes: "For Montaigne, it is in our lack of understanding of the actions of animals and of the languages they may well be using that the border between us and animals must lie. This border, however, is not strictly a discernible one; it is more of a limit that indicates a gap, an extension of the gap that often enough makes a human being incomprehensible to another and even to him/herself. . . . It is a border in constant flux with respect to human understanding, as is reason itself."[17] So it is just possible, indeed likely, that the difference between ourselves and animals is cultural rather than strictly biological, and therefore open to specific judgments as to how we should live rather than to logical determinations as to what goes where within ready-made conceptual frameworks. In this event empathy trumps cognition in our dealings with others, whether human or otherwise, which is why the question of suffering looms so large in long-standing controversies concerning our responsibility to and for others, however these others are conceived.[18]

So much (for the moment) for the upper limit. What about the lower? "The lower limit upon humanity," Cavell says, "is marked by the passage into inhumanity. Its signal is horror" (CR, 434).

> What is the object of horror? At what do we tremble in this way? Fear is of danger; terror is of violence, of the violence I might do or that might be done me. I can be terrified of thunder but not horrified by it. And isn't it the case that not the human horrifies me, but the inhuman, the monstrous? Very well. But only what is human can be inhuman. —Can only the human be monstrous? If something is monstrous, and we do not believe that there are monsters, then only the human is a candidate for the monstrous. (CR, 418)

"Can only the human be monstrous?" The question has some application to Kafka's ape, who is perhaps never more human (because never more inhuman) than when he is unable to look his mistress in the eye, with its "insane look of the bewildered half-broken animal." Being human means the power to grant being human, but the experience of flesh (sexuality, bewilderment, my own as well as the other's) is a limit-experience: on which side do I fall? What if the ape's mistress had looked at him with a cool nod or smile of recognition?

"Horror," says Cavell, "is the title I am giving to the perception of the precariousness of human identity, to the perception that it may be lost or invaded, that we may be, or may become, something other than we are, or take ourselves for; that our origins as human beings need accounting for, and are unaccountable" (CR, 418–19).[19] Horror in this sense is what is inspired by (or what inspires the social production of) outcasts—those (Cavell mentions Oedipus, who by now perhaps comes too easily to mind) who violate, and so help to define, the boundaries we have drawn that separate us from the other (Agamben's wolf-man, for example). But what interests Cavell is, interestingly, horror as a species of self-experience: "The outcast is a figure of pity and horror; different from ourselves, and not different. . . . We should try looking at him as a figure of horror to himself" (*CR*, 420–21). Which is how one could, arguably, look at Kafka's ape, who might, after all, have regarded his mistress's dilemma with some compassion (that is, humanely: helped her out, or along the path on which she finds herself; but of course we don't know her story).

Opposed to horror, in Cavell's thinking, is empathy, which is what I feel, not when I identify you *as* a human being, but when I identify *with* you—a capacity for fellow-feeling that I have, naturally, when it comes to my dog, James (in contrast to some humorless academics I can think of). Cavell wonders what would it be for empathy to go astray—"You might, for all I know, be a mutation, or a perfected automaton or an android, or a golem, or some other species of alien" (*CR*, 422): in other words, disguised, an impersonator of the human, like Kafka's ape, with whom Kafka enables us to empathize, if with some disquiet, since the ironic thrust of Kafka's story is to disqualify us, his readers, as edifying creatures (what's so great about being human if an ape could do it? what's so great about it if an ape proves to be superior to us in the order of culture or good breeding? or capable, as only humans are, of bestiality?).

Cavell shares with Kafka something like a philosophical disquiet (or possibly a Montaigne-like skepticism) concerning the criteria—or the powers of reason—available to us when it comes to picking something out, or responding to it, as a human being or, more aptly, as a fellow creature. "Obviously," Cavell writes, continuing his thought experiment concerning horror and empathy, "you can never be certain that other human beings exist, for any one you single out may, for all you know, be something other than you imagine, perhaps a human, probably a human if you like, but possibly a mutation, and just possibly an automaton, a zombie . . . The world is what it is. And whatever it is, so far as you take it as inhabited by candidates for the human, you are empathetically projecting. This means that you cannot rule out the nonhuman (or human non-being) possibility" (*CR*, 423–24).

The idea of a *candidate* for the human is worth a second thought, particularly against the background of narratives, like Cavell's story of the craftsman and the friend, in which an artifact approaches a threshold of being human and requires only a final and imperceptible alteration, not so much in its material or its machinery as in how it is regarded, as in the Pygmalion story, in which the artist's lunatic love for his creation moves Venus to incarnate the statue with life. Here one thinks of "The First Appearance of the Machine in Humanity," which is the title of a chapter from Villiers de l'Isle-Adam's *L'Ève future* (1886), a novel in which Thomas Alva Edison, the genius of Menlo Park, creates a "female" android named Hadaly that is fully conscious, able to hold intelligent conversations, yet is not a finished piece of work. What is missing is someone who will "animate" her affectively by responding to her as if she were human. Whereupon Lord Celian Ewald unexpectedly arrives; he is, as it happens, in a dilemma that has him on the verge of suicide. He is passionate about Miss Alicia Clary, an actress and a staggering beauty who, sadly, possesses (or is possessed by) a thoroughly obnoxious personality. Fair without, foul within, as Shakespeare once phrased the paradox. By contrast Hadaly, because she is electro-magnetic all the way through, "offers none of the disagreeable impressions that one gets from watching the *vital processes* of our own organism."[20] So, on Lord Ewald's behalf, Edison sets to work, photosculpting Alicia Clary's magnificent flesh and fitting it neatly onto Hadaly's wireworks, thus to transform the android into a creature who transcends the defective original—a more suitable candidate for the human, so one might put it, than the merely human itself. Incarnated now in Miss Clary's image, Hadaly pleads with Lord Ewald: "You ask, 'Who I am?' My being in this low world depends, *for you at least*, only on your free will. Attribute a being to me, affirm that I am! Reinforce me with yourself. And then suddenly I will come to life under your eyes, to precisely the extent that your creative Good Will has penetrated me. Like a true woman, I will be for you only as you desire me. . . . My ethereal flesh, which awaits but the breath of your spirit to become living, my voice within which the soul of harmony lies captive, my undying constancy . . . " (*TE*, 199–200). Happily, Lord Ewald is able to overcome his common sense ("Since when has

God permitted machines to usurp the right of speech?" [*TE*, 201]). As he himself puts it, he "resign[s] from the human race" (*TE*, 204), as if the embrace of a cyborg entailed the repudiation of the very idea of being human.[21]

Which may leave us, who- or whatever we are, not knowing where we are. After all, it appears that in zones of indistinction the very idea of being human, or anything at all, loses its application. In such zones, creatures of whatever origin are, so to speak, free of their origins, which is to say free from the taxonomies that separate them from others—free, in other words, from what Giorgio Agamben calls "the anthropological machine":

> *Homo sapiens* . . . is neither a clearly defined species nor a substance; it is, rather, a machine or device for producing the recognition of the human. . . . It is an optical machine constructed of a series of mirrors in which man, looking at himself, sees his own image always already deformed in the features of an ape. *Homo* is a constitutively "anthropomorphous" animal (that is, "resembling man," according to the term that Linnaeus constantly uses until the tenth edition of his *Systema*), who must recognize himself in a non-man in order to be human.[22]

Desubjectivation

(MICHEL FOUCAULT'S
AESTHETICS OF EXPERIENCE)

> From the idea that the self is not given to us,
> I think there is only one practical consequence:
> we have to create ourselves as a work of art.
> —Michael Foucault, "On the Genealogy of Ethics"
>
> I call experience the voyage to the end of the possible of man.
> —Georges Bataille, *Inner Experience*

Becoming Something Other

Michel Foucault began writing his *Histoire de sexualité* (1976–84) as, arguably, a social constructionist—someone who believes that our cognitive powers and capacities for experience are socially formed—and he ended as someone who believes that we not only can but should work on ourselves in order to form ourselves as ethical subjects (and even "create ourselves as a work of art").[1] The question is: What to make of this project? For example, what can "subject" mean at this stage of the game? With Foucault, after all, there is some doubt as to what, exactly, human subjectivity could consist in—supposing the word "human" doesn't beg the question, since for Foucault, as for many others of his generation, "a systematic skepticism with respect to all anthropological universals" is a point of departure.[2] We are the others of each other, not of any One.

But who is *we*? Foucault's early answer, derived from his reading of Nietzsche, Georges Bataille, and Maurice Blanchot, is "that we are difference, that our reason is the difference of discourses, our history the difference of times, ourselves the difference of masks (*AS*, 172–73/*AK*, 131)." Of course, *difference* is most famous as a concept in critiques of metaphysics, representation, and subject-centered rationality. Foucault seldom uses the term, but his use of it here is close to what Gilles Deleuze calls "difference in itself"—an anarchic difference on the hither side of logical relations of identity, opposition, analogy, and resemblance:

> Difference must become the element, the ultimate unity [that is, singular and irreducible]; it must therefore refer to other differences which never identify it but rather differenciate it [where *différencier*, to make or become different, is to be distinguished from the mathematical operation, *différentier*]. Each term of a series, being already a difference, must be put into a variable relation with other terms, thereby constituting other series devoid of center and convergence. Divergence and decentering must be affirmed in the series itself. *Every object, every thing, must see its own identity swallowed up in difference, each being no more than a difference between differences* [my emphasis]. Difference must be shown *differing*. We know that modern art tends to realize these conditions: in this sense it becomes a veritable theater of metamorphoses and permutations. A theater where nothing is fixed, a labyrinth without a thread (Ariadne has hung herself). *The work of art leaves the domain of representation in order to become "experience."* (my emphasis)[3]

Difference here cannot be relativized to sameness. Difference is non-identity, or what Blanchot calls "a relation of the third kind," a "relation without relation" ("a relation we are designating as multiple only inasmuch as it is not determined by the One").[4]

For Foucault difference in itself as a condition of subjectivity would be something excessive or irreducible with respect to processes of social formation. It would be an indeterminate and anonymous remainder, an incarcerable surplus—a self figured not substantively as *moi* but reflexively as *soi*. Our relation to this self—*rapport à soi*—is what Foucault calls "ethics" (but also "hermeneutics" and, to add to the complexity, "aesthetics").[5] It presupposes a shift from the third- to the first-person perspective, where, importantly, the first-person perspective is not that of the logical subject—the universalizable "I think"—but that of the singular subject of *experience*.[6]

What kind of experience? In what follows I would like to determine what this turn toward singularity or non-identity in Foucault's thinking might mean with respect to being a subject of experience—where (so it appears) experience is not *Erlebnis*, lived or shared experience, but *Erfahrung*: experience as passage, ordeal, reversal, perhaps even annihilation. The term should be understood with Hegel in mind, particularly this famous passage from his introduction to *The Phenomenology of Spirit*:

> Whatever is confined within the limits of natural life cannot by its own efforts go beyond its immediate existence; but it is driven beyond it by something else, and this uprooting entails its death. Consciousness, however, is explicitly the *Notion* [*Begriff*] of itself. Hence it is something that goes beyond limits, and since these limits are its own, it is something that goes beyond itself. With the positing of a single particular the beyond is also established for consciousness, even if it is only *alongside* the limited object as in the case of spatial intuition. Thus consciousness suffers this violence [*Gewalt*] at its own hands: it spoils its own limited satisfaction.[7]

I think that experience as an event in which one goes beyond limits and overcomes oneself (even to the point of suffering "violence" at one's own hands) comes close to what Foucault may have had in mind *even while* speaking (in very different terms) of "working on oneself" and "creating oneself as a work of art."

Which is to say that how to understand Foucault's later thinking remains, not just an open question, but maybe an unanswerable one. His writings do not develop straightforwardly but are a tangle of shifts, breaks, and competing programs of research. His terms and concepts (particularly "aesthetics" and "experience") are never stable, and of course, because of his untimely death, his thinking with respect to one's self-relation came to a stop rather than to an end, leaving us finally with bits and pieces to assemble. At the same time, however, the internal complexity of his work is not accidental. On my reading, Foucault is a modernist in the tradition of Nietzsche, Bataille, and Blanchot—

namely, someone who rejects repetition in all of its forms and manifestations, which means a rejection of the very notion of "adherence" with respect to norms, models, concepts, distinctions, principles, and rules—and in particular the rule of identity. In this tradition nonlinearity overturns consecutive reasoning. What sets Foucault apart from his predecessors—or where he follows them most creatively (Bataille in particular)—is in his attempt to develop a concept of freedom that is coherent with this refusal of normative constructions: he is someone who thinks that we are capable of "practicing" freedom as an essentially anarchic form of life (*DEII*, 1528–29/E, 282–83).[8] An anarchic form of life enjoys a shortfall of criteria; it is one in which nothing is settled in advance, and the idea is to keep things (and oneself) in motion.

As Foucault says, "My way of not being the same is, by definition, the most singular part of what I am."[9] The paradox here echoes Rimbaud's watchword, *Je est un autre*, as well as Theodor Adorno's antinomic definition of the task of modern art: "To make things of which we do not know what they are."[10] And keep in mind Deleuze's figure of the work of art, cited above, as a "theater of metamorphosis and permutation," where nothing remains "fixed," and where "work" is not an object but an event—an *experience*. In his book on Foucault, Deleuze writes: "The struggle for a modern subjectivity passes through a resistance to the two present forms of subjection, the one consisting of individualizing ourselves on the basis of constraints of power, the other of attracting each individual to a known and recognizable identity, fixed once and for all. The struggle for subjectivity presents itself, therefore, as the right to difference, variation and metamorphosis."[11] Or even, as the elusive, reclusive Blanchot says in his essay on Foucault, "the right to disappear."[12]

Just so, Foucault's idea, as we shall see, is to avoid, not just subjection, but *subjectivation*: being made into something familiar—something recognizable (and controllable). In an interview in which he remained "anonymous," "The Masked Philosopher," Foucault said: "The movement by which, not without effort and uncertainty, dreams and illusions, one detaches oneself from what is accepted as true and seeks other rules—that is philosophy. The displacement and transformation of frameworks of thinking [*des cadres de pensée*], the changing of received values and all the work that has been done to think otherwise, to do something else, to become something other than what one is [*pour devenir autre que ce qu'on est*]—that too is philosophy" (*DEII*, 929/*E*, 327). Becoming "something other than what one is" is a purely fugitive project, one that is purposefully without definition or period—in becoming *other*, there is no saying what one becomes, because there is no *what*, as if the goal were to become, as Giorgio Agamben says of the modern artist, "the man without content, who has no other identity than a perpetual emerging out of the nothingness of expression and no other ground than this incomprehensible station on the hither side of himself."[13] If "himself" is the word.

Bio-Power and the Abnormals

As for becoming familiar: the (by now well-known) thesis of the first volume of *The History of Sexuality* (1976) is that modernity—Western or European culture since the late seventeenth century—has treated sex not as a secret to be kept but as an object of knowledge around which a whole disciplinary system of discourses and practices has developed, a system of "technologies" in which "sex becomes a matter that required the social body as a whole, and virtually all of its individuals, to place itself under surveillance" (*HSI*, 116/ *VS*, 155). However, these "technologies" are not just disciplinary or punitive; they are practices which, during the nineteenth century, the ruling upper and middle classes began to apply not to others (the working classes, the peasantry) but to themselves. "What was involved," Foucault writes, "was not an asceticism, not a renunciation of pleasure or a disqualification of the flesh, but on the contrary an intensification of the body, a problematization of health and its operational terms: it was a question of techniques for the maximizing of life. The primary concern was not repression of the sex of classes to be exploited, but rather the body, vigor, longevity, progeniture, and descent of the classes that 'ruled'" (*HSI*, 122–23/*VS*, 162). The idea was to bring sex under control, not in order to stifle it, but in order to make it productive.

Specifically, the bourgeoisie began to understand itself within the context of the new science of biology. Biology became part of its self-governance.

Whereas traditional sovereignty consists in power over life and death—a juridical power which expresses itself through killing or the threat of killing—in the nineteenth century a new form of power arises aimed at life: "Western man was gradually learning what it meant to be a living species in a living world, to have a body, conditions of existence, probabilities of life, an individual and collective welfare, conditions that could be modified. . . . Power would no longer be dealing simply with legal subjects over whom the ultimate dominion was death, but with living beings, and the mastery it would be able to exercise over them would have to be applied at the level of life itself" (*HSI*, 142–43/*VS*, 187). Foucault calls this "bio-power" (*bio-pouvoir*): "If one can apply the term bio-*history* to the pressures through which movements of life and the processes of history interfere with one another, one would have to speak of *bio-power* [*bio-politique*] to designate what brought life and its mechanisms into the realm of explicit calculations and made knowledge-power an agent of transformation of human life" (*HSI*, 143/*VS*, 188).

(In "Rules for the Human Zoo," Peter Sloterdijk refers to this as "the domestication of man," or *bioselection*, in which human beings of a certain order now come to breed themselves as they do other animals. Bourgeois bio-power is simply the forerunner of *biotechnology* or genetic engineering.)[14]

What interests Foucault, however, is not just the social formation of bourgeois subjects but the castoffs of this breeding process. The normalization of "heterosexual monogamy," for example, entailed the investigation of individuals who were, in various ways, borderline, anomalous, or impossible with respect to the norm: "What came under scrutiny was the sexuality of children, mad men and women, and criminals; the sensuality of those who did not like the opposite sex; reveries, obsessions, petty manias, or great transports of rage. It was time for all these figures, scarcely noticed in the past, to step forward and speak, to make the difficult confession of what they were" (*HSI*, 38–39/*VS*, 53). A new species came into existence—"the abnormals," as Foucault calls them.

Foucault devoted his course of lectures in 1974–75 to the genealogical development of the medieval "monster" into the juridical-medical figure of the "abnormal."[15] But his principal object of inquiry here was "the power of normalization"—the psychiatric "technology of abnormality"—rather than the abnormals as individual subjects.[16] The question of what it would be "for all of these figures, scarcely noticed in the past, *to step forward and speak*," remained, for the time being, in suspension.

In fact eight years passed between the first volume of the *History of Sexuality* and the second and third volumes. In a separately published preface to the second volume, *L'usage de plaisirs*, Foucault indicates that his earlier study of the history of madness had left him "unsatisfied" because of "its theoretical weakness in elaborating the notion of experience" (*DEII*, 1398/*E*, 200). Nor did his studies of sickness and criminality, concerned as they may have been with "the very historicity of forms of experience" (*DEII*, 1398/*E*, 200), really take up the question of how "individual and collective experiences arise from singular forms of thought—that is, from what constitutes the subject in its relations to the true, to rules, to itself" (*DEII*, 1400/*E*, 202). To the question of knowledge and power Foucault now adds what he calls the "third matrix"—"the modality of relation to the self" (*DEII*, 1402/*E*, 204)—which, he says, came naturally into the foreground with the study of the historical formation and deployment of sexuality. The question is: What sort of relation is this relation of the self to itself? It is this question, Foucault says, that forced him to break with his "chronological outline" (*DEII*, 1402/*E*, 204) and to transform his project from a history of sexuality as a discursive epoch of modernity into an analysis of "what is termed 'the subject,'" and "to look for the forms and modalities of the relation to self by which the individual constitutes and recognizes himself *qua* subject" (*HSII*, 6/*UP*, 12–13).

Experience as Desubjectivation

In his introduction to the second volume of his *History of Sexuality* Foucault says that his purpose in volume 1 was not to write "a history of sexual behaviors and practices" but to study the theoretical and practical context—the forms of knowledge, the rules and norms, the religious, pedagogical, juridical, and medical institutions—in which the term "sexuality" and its various embodied forms were first deployed. To which he then adds this modification—and notice the shift from the third to the first person: "In short, it was a matter of seeing how an 'experience' came to be constituted in modern Western societies, an experience that caused individuals to recognize themselves as subjects of a 'sexuality'" (*HSII*, 10/*UP*, 4). "Experience" was slow to become a term of art in Foucault's lexicon.[17] When in 1961 he speaks of the "experience of madness," for example, he does not mean a first-person experience but the experience of an observer, whether a Renaissance humanist, an eighteenth-century philosophe, or a nineteenth-century psychiatrist (*FD*, 10/*MC*, xii). Meanwhile, by my rough reckoning the word "experience" occurs only once in volume 1 of *The History of Sexuality*, where it is nestled like a seed in the chapter "Scientia Sexualis." Here Foucault makes the interesting observation that, whereas in Eastern cultures the discourse of sex takes the form of the *ars erotica*, in the West (in the early modern period) it was made into a scientific object that discloses itself, paradoxically, in the form of the confession:

> This was an important time. . . . It was a time when the most singular pleasures were called upon to pronounce a discourse of truth concerning themselves, a discourse which had to model itself after that which spoke, not of sin and salvation, but of bodies and life processes—the discourse of science. It was enough to make one's voice tremble, for an improbable thing was then taking shape: a confessional science, a science which relied on a many-sided extortion, and took for its object what was unmentionable but admitted to nonetheless. The scientific discourse was scandalized, or in any case repelled, when it had to take charge of this whole discourse from below. (*HSI*, 64/*VS*, 80)

A "discourse from below" is not, however, autonomous. Foucault stresses that "the confession is a ritual of discourse in which the speaking subject is also the subject of the statement; it is also a ritual that unfolds within a power relationship, for one does not confess without the presence (or virtual presence) of a partner who is not simply the interlocutor but the authority who requires the confession" (*HSI*, 61/*VS*, 82–83). But for all of that the one who confesses remains the subject of an experience—an experience of being "something other."

In "Lives of Infamous Men" (1977), the introduction to an anthology of official capsule narratives of lowly miscreants "at the point of their instantaneous contact with power," Foucault imagines the following reproach to his obsessive interest in power: "I will be told: 'That's so like you, always with the same inability to cross the line, to pass to the other side, to listen and convey the language that comes from elsewhere or from below; always the same choice, on the side of power, of what it says or causes to be said. Why not go listen to these lives where they speak in their own voice?'" (*DEII*, 241/*P*, 161). In fact, attending to such voices was what Foucault began to do about the time he was finishing *La volonté de savoir*. In 1973 he published the first of two editions of "discourses from below," *Moi, Pierre Rivière, ayant égorgé ma mère, ma sœur et mon frère: Une cas de parricide au XIXe siècle*, the memoir of a man who, after murdering members of his family, fled to the forest where he "wandered for a long time, like a man without culture, an animal without instinct, that is to say, like something which, specifically, did not exist, a mythical being, a monstrous being impossible to define because it does not belong to any identifiable order."[18] This publication was followed in 1978 by *Herculine Barbin, dite Alexina B.*, the autobiography or memoir of a hermaphrodite who was identified as female at birth (1828), who was raised in a boarding school for girls and taught in a school for young women before being officially declared a man by the courts in 1860—before, in other words, being "normalized" and, paradoxically, *confined* in a way she had not been during her life as a student and teacher.

In his introduction to this text Foucault writes:

> Alexina wrote her memoirs about that life once her new identity had been discovered and established. Her "true" and "definitive" identity. But it is clear she did not write them from the point of view of that sex which had at last been brought to light. It is not a man who is speaking, trying to recall his sensations and his life as they were at the time when he was not yet "himself." When Alexina composed her memoirs, she was not far from suicide; for herself, she was still without a definite sex, but she was deprived of the delights she experienced in not having one, or in not entirely having the same sex as the

girls among whom she lived and whom she loved and desired so much. And what she evokes in her past is *the happy limbo of a non-identity* [my emphasis], which was paradoxically protected by the life of those closed, narrow, and intimate societies where one has the strange happiness, which is at the same time obligatory and forbidden, of being acquainted with only one sex.[19]

Foucault reads Herculine's memoir as a testimony to the freedom (the "happy limbo") of non-identity, but her sexual heterogeneity also recalls the form of experience that Foucault took up earlier in his essay on Bataille, "Preface to Transgression" (1963), where transgression is not simply a violation of statutes but is rather what Bataille calls an "inner experience," an experience of pure exteriority that turns the subject inside out, exposing it, paradoxically, to what cannot be thought, like the God of the mystics, whom Bataille secularizes into the "path of non-knowledge" (*ExI*, 65/*IE*, 51). Experience is an experience of being laid bare (as in ecstasy) before this *inconnu*. Bataille calls experience "a voyage to the end of the possible of man" (*ExI*, 19/*IE*, 7) and speaks of living life at *"the extreme limit of the 'possible'"* (*ExI*, 52/*IE*, 39). Blanchot, elucidating Bataille, refers to it as a "limit-experience": experience which can no longer be framed within the categories of subject and object, same and other, identity and difference—an experience of being no one (*EI*, 304–5/*IC*, 205).

In his essay on Blanchot, "La pensée dehors" (1966), Foucault gives us a genealogy of this extreme experience (Sade, Hölderlin, Mallarmé, Nietzsche) which Blanchot explores from the reflexive standpoint of the first person in his *récits*, with their experiences of waiting, forgetting, weakness, anonymity, affliction, insomnia, dying: events that occur interminably within horizons of empty rooms, windows, hallways (figures of the *il y a*).[20] One's relation to oneself in this experience is a non-relation: a relation of the third kind in which one is neither the one nor the other of any possible term but simply *le Neutre*:

> From a verbal point of view [Blanchot writes], the unknown is neuter. The discretion of the French language, which does not possess a neuter gender, is awkward but finally not without its virtue, for what belongs to the neuter is not a third gender opposed to the other two and constituting for reason a

determined class of existents or beings. The neuter is that which cannot be assigned to any genre whatsoever: the non-general, the non-generic, as well as the non-particular. It refuses to belong to the category of subject as much as it does to that of object. And this does not simply mean that it is still undetermined and as though hesitating between the two, but rather that the neuter supposes another relation depending neither on objective conditions nor on subjective dispositions. (*EI*, 440/*IC*, 299)

To which he adds: "The neutral is thus constantly expelled from our languages and our truths" (*EI*, 440/*IC*, 299). It is the an-archic as such. In Foucault's idiom, it is what is absolutely refractory to normalization and, indeed, to rule of identity in all of its applications.

In an interview published in 1980, Foucault distinguishes between two conceptions of experience. There is the phenomenological tradition (in which Foucault himself was schooled), in which experience means "bringing a reflective gaze on some object of 'lived experience.'" By contrast, for "Nietzsche, Bataille, and Blanchot, experience is trying to reach a certain point in life that is as close as possible to the 'unlivable,' to that which can't be lived through. What is required is the maximum of intensity and the maximum of impossibility at the same time." Phenomenology "attempts to recapture the meaning of everyday experience in order to rediscover the sense in which the subject that I am is indeed responsible, in its transcendental functions, for founding that experience together with its meanings. On the other hand, in Nietzsche, Bataille, and Blanchot, experience has the function of wrenching the subject from itself, of seeing to it that the subject is no longer itself, or that it is brought to its annihilation or its dissolution. This is a project of desubjectivation [*une enterprise de dé-subjectivation*]" (*DEII*, 862/*P*, 241).[21]

Termination

One cannot help noticing the violence of Foucault's language: "Experience is trying to reach a certain point in life that is as close as possible to the 'unlivable'"; it "has the function of wrenching the subject from itself, of seeing to it that the subject is no longer itself, or that it is brought to its annihilation or its dissolution." What Foucault has in mind is something more radical than a mere "critique of the subject." The idea is not simply to call a concept into question (as in "death of the author"). As Foucault says: "Such an operation would be meaningless if it remained limited to speculation. Calling the subject into question means that one would have to experience something leading to its actual destruction, its decomposition, its explosion, its conversion into something else"—something inaccessible to definition, or maybe even to any intelligible narrative (*DEII*, 867/*P*, 247).

Destruction, decomposition, explosion: this indeterminacy or, more accurately, termination of the subject is not easy to reconcile with notions of self-formation, much less an "aesthetics of existence" in which one creates oneself as a work of art. The principal difficulty is that there are (characteristically) conflicting, not to say contradictory, conceptions of "aesthetics" in Foucault's thinking, only the first of which has received much attention. The third volume of *The History of Sexuality* concerns the ancient Greek and Roman practice of *epimeleia heautou*, "care of the self (*soi*)," which presupposes a conversion of oneself to oneself (*conversio ad se* [*HSIII*, 81/*CS*, 65]), a turning of one's eyes or one's concentration upon oneself that has a number of dimensions—a medical dimension of care for one's body, a political and juridical concern for self-mastery, and (most important) an *aesthetics of pleasure*. *Conversio*, Foucault emphasizes, is basically "an ethics of control [*éthique de la maîtrise*]" in which "one exercises over oneself an authority that nothing limits or threatens" (*HSIII*, 82/*CS*, 65). But more than this, "the relation to self is also defined as a concrete relationship enabling one to delight in oneself, as in a thing one both possesses and has before one's eyes" (*HSIII*, 82/*CS*, 65). One's experience of the self is an experience of pleasure—a pleasure, to be sure, that is very different from the turbulent and short-lived pleasures of the *aphrodisia*: not voluptuous or sensual pleasure but rather something contemplative, a pleasure of self-reflection in which one is entirely at home with oneself and without need for or dependence on others or on anything outside of oneself (*HSIII*, 83–84/*CS*, 66). It is pleasure that presupposes freedom—and a very traditional conception of freedom: namely, autonomy.

Let us call this Foucault's Apollonian side. But *desubjectivation* entails a radically different conception: freedom, not just from others, but from oneself, or even from being anything like a *self* or entity of any sort. Pierre Hadot and Michael Ure have criticized Foucault for the way he "modernizes" the ancients, importing into Greek and Roman ethics a narcissistic self derived variously from Baudelaire, Nietzsche, and Wilde.[22] However, desubjectivation seems rather closer to Baudelaire's Apache than to the figure of the Dandy.[23] More to the point, the later Foucault (or at least part of him) is after something like an aesthetics of the sublime, where what one experiences is "beyond pleasure," which is how psychoanalysts like Jacques Lacan characterize *jouissance*, in which the subject approaches "a center of incandescence or an absolute zero that is physically unbearable."[24]

Here one should try to imagine the experience of violence of a kind reflected in Bataille's paradox of gaiety in the face of death:

> If I envisage death gaily, it is not that I too say, in turning away from what is frightening: "it is nothing" or "it is false." On the contrary, gaiety, connected with the work of death, causes me anguish: ultimately, gay anguish, anguished gaiety cause me, in a feverish chill, "absolute dismemberment," where it is my joy that finally tears me apart, but where dejection would follow joy were I not torn all the way to the end, immeasurably.[25]

Foucault's concept of desubjectivation clearly resonates with Bataille's "practice of joy before death"—a kind of *thanaesthetics*—in which one's life is "fulfilled in rending agony" (*VE*, 236), an idea that Bataille constructed from a number of contexts: Nietzsche's idea of self-overcoming, various mystical traditions with their premium on the loss of self, as well as anthropological descriptions of sacrificial rituals in which dismemberment is represented as a form of ecstasy—self-annihilation as transcendence.[26]

As Bataille says in *Inner Experience*: "If one proceeds right to the end, one must efface oneself, undergo solitude, suffer severely from it, renounce being *recognized*: to be as though absent, insane over this, to undergo things without will and without hope, to be elsewhere" (*ExI*, 179 / *IE*, 155). Naturally

Dionysus comes to mind: "Through loss man can regain the free movement of the universe, he can dance and swirl in the full rapture of those great swarms of stars. But he must, in the violent expenditure of self, perceive that he breathes in the power of death."[27]

Let me conclude by pursuing this antinomic line of thought to its end. In his "Preface" to *Madame Edwarda*, one of his "erotic" fictions, Bataille writes:

> The act whereby being—existence—is bestowed upon us is an unbearable surpassing of being, an act no less unbearable than that of dying. And since, in death, being is taken away from us at the same time it is given to us, we must seek for it in the feeling of dying, in those unbearable moments when it seems to us that we are dying, because the existence in us, during these interludes, exists through nothing but a sustaining and ruinous excess, when the fullness of horror and joy coincide.[28]

Jean-Luc Nancy says Bataille "had no *concept* of the subject" (*CD*, 18/*InC*, 24). In fact, Bataille's conception of the subject derives from Hegel's idea that man becomes what he is by negating whatever he is not—the world of mere things, including his own body or animal nature.[29] But Bataille reverses this dialectic of negation. His position is that the loss or *expenditure* (*dépense*) of subjectivity is an achievement of sovereignty, where sovereignty (recall Tournier's *Vendredi*) is not mastery but freedom from every form of subordination, including that of self-possession or self-rule—the "ethics of control" that, in Bataille's scheme, one abandons in the "ruinous" excesses of eroticism (incest, sadism, defilement, or whatever is heterogeneous with respect to the bourgeois order of things).[30] If, following Hegel, *man creates himself through his prohibitions* (*AS*, 53), then Bataille's sovereignty is "the negation of prohibition" (*AS*, 254)—*the end of the possible of man*.

4

Becoming-Animal
(SOME SIMPLE WAYS)

Nomads

In *A Thousand Plateaus* Gilles Deleuze and Felix Guattari say that they "believe in the existence of very special becomings-animal traversing human beings and sweeping them away, affecting the animal no less than the human" (*MP*, 290/ *TP*, 237). What sort of metamorphosis might this be (and how exactly might it affect the animal)? Deleuze and Guattari are notorious improvisers of concepts, which are not always meant to be clear (since for them a concept is never exactly "about" something), but what they have in mind may be something like this. At a certain level of organization each of us is a "human" being, but as we descend to ground level—say to the level of the singular and irreducible, or the level of experience—it becomes increasingly difficult, and even undesirable, to apply concepts and distinctions of any sort. The word "man" is imperative, not nominative or descriptive; it is an *order-word*—"Be a man!" ("Language is not life; it gives orders. Life does not speak, it listens and waits" [*MP*, 96/ *TP*, 76].) In the terms of art that Deleuze and Guattari characteristically use, becoming-animal is a movement from major (the constant) to minor (the variable); it is a deterritorialization in which a subject no longer occupies a realm of stability and identity but is instead folded imperceptibly into a movement or into an amorphous *legion* whose mode of existence is nomadic or, alternatively, whose "structure" is rhizomatic rather than arborescent, that is, restless, insomniac, or in flight rather than settled, upright, or at one with itself and at peace with others. ("We're tired of trees. We should stop believing in trees, roots, and radicles. They've made us suffer too much. All of arborescent culture is founded on them, from biology to linguistics" [*MP*, 24/*TP*, 15].) It is a movement from molar to molecular combinations, from unity to complexity, that is, from organization to anarchy, which is the mode of being of whatever is uncontainable within an order of things, as in the case of the War Machine vis-à-vis the State.

The war machine is the anarchic or nomadic group in its primordial form, "irreducible to the State apparatus . . . outside its sovereignty and prior to its law: it comes from elsewhere" (*MP*, 435/*TP*, 352). The war machine is a condition of pure exteriority, and remains so even when the state tries to incorporate it into itself in the form of an army. "The State has no war machine of its own; it can only appropriate one in the form of a military institution, one that will continually cause it problems. This explains the mistrust States have toward their military institutions, in that the military institution inherits the extrinsic war machine" (*MP*, 439/*TP*, 355). The war machine is subversive of every integrity, like the Amazons in Kleist's *Penthesilea*, "stateless women-people whose justice, religion, and loves are organized uniquely in a war mode"—that is, there is nothing that is not their enemy: "They sweep away everything in their path" (*MP*, 439/*TP*, 355). This is because the warrior "is like a pure and immeasurable multiplicity, the pack, an irruption of the ephemeral and the power of metamorphosis" (*MP*, 435/*TP*, 352): in other words, elusive and unsettling, a roving band, which is the figure of becoming in itself.[1]

Becoming is a pure event, a simultaneity "whose characteristic is to elude the present. Insofar as it eludes the present, becoming does not tolerate the separation or the distinction of before and after, or of past and future. It pertains to the essence of becoming to move and to pull in both directions at once."[2] Becoming cannot be plotted with points of reference. There are many kinds of becoming, including (as we shall see) becoming-woman, but nomadic movement without determination is the key to this event. In their book, *Kafka: Toward a Minor Literature*, Deleuze and Guattari write:

> To become animal is to participate in movement, to stake out a path of escape in all its positivity, to cross a threshold, to reach a continuum of intensities that are valuable only in themselves, to find a world of pure intensities *where all forms come undone, as do all the significations, signifiers, and signifieds*, to the benefit of an unformed matter of deterritorialized flux, of nonsignifying signs. Kafka's animals never refer to a mythology or to archetypes but correspond

solely to new levels, zones of liberated intensities where contents free themselves from their forms as well as from their expressions, from the signifier that formalized them. (13; my emphasis)

An intensity is something like a moving line without boundaries or points along the way, a pure difference without structure or definition— whence "all forms come undone." However, the anarchy of becoming is not just logical or formal; it has a social (or maybe *asocial*) significance. "A becoming-animal," Deleuze and Guattari say, "always involves a pack, a band, a population, a peopling, in short a multiplicity" (*MP*, 292/*TP*, 239). The morphology of this metamorphosis is captured in vampire stories in which the bitten subject is drained away by a kind of infection or contagion, and in turn is no longer containable within the alternatives of living and nonliving, human and nonhuman, man and beast, but who nevertheless remains abroad in the world, roaming in swarms or bands that consume whatever is around them. (Hence the team or the club, which frequently identifies itself in the name of an animal, is always on the perimeter of the social order, as on a line between a productive group and the gregarious gathering.)

De Anomalia

This does not mean that someone who runs with the pack becomes no one, a face in the crowd (*das Man*). On the contrary, in every pack there is (one is) always "a leader of the pack," except that such a figure is not so much an individual as an anomaly, a heteroclite entity, an *aliquid*. "What exactly is the nature of the anomalous?" Deleuze and Guattari ask (*MP*, 298–99/*TP*, 244). Etymologically the anomalous is the uneven or the irregular, the one that does not fit. "The anomalous is neither an individual nor a species; it has only affects, it has neither familiar or subjectified feelings, nor specific characteristics. Human tenderness [or anything like empathy] is as foreign as human classification" (*MP*, 299/*TP*, 244–45). Deleuze and Guattari refer us to H. P. Lovecraft's Thing, "which arrives and passes at the edge, 'teeming, seething, swelling, foaming, spreading like an infectious disease, this nameless horror'" (*MP*, 299/*TP*, 245). The anomalous *Thing* is situated at a borderline, rather like Maurice Blanchot's *le Neutre*, the Other Man (*Autrui*) who is outside all contexts and horizons and, indeed, outside all possibilities of naming and comprehension, who marks a limit of cognition and representation as the *foreign* as such, and who therefore "risks being always Other than man, close to what cannot be close to me: close to death, close to the night, and certainly as repulsive as anything that comes to me from these regions without horizon" (*EI*, 103/*IC*, 72). Repulsive—but we must imagine someone who is monstrous because featureless.

To explore (or expand) this domain Deleuze and Guattari do not hesitate to invoke the figure of the sorcerer. "Sorcerers have always held the anomalous position, at the edge of the field or woods" (*MP*, 301/*TP*, 246), at the opening of the nether world inhabited by demons capable of taking or inhabiting any shape, modes or forces of indeterminate flesh:

> It can be said that becoming-animal is an affair of sorcery because (1) it implies an initial relation of alliance with a demon; (2) the demon functions as the borderline of the animal pack, into which the human being passes or in which his or her becoming takes place, by contagion; (3) this becoming itself implies a second alliance, with another human group; (4) this new borderline between the two groups guides the contagion of animal and human being within the pack. There is an entire politics of becomings-animal, as well as a politics of sorcery, which is elaborated in assemblages that are neither those of the family nor of religion nor of the State. Instead, they express minoritarian groups, or groups that are oppressed, prohibited, in revolt, or always on the fringe of recognized institutions, groups all the more secret for being intrinsic, in other words, anomic. (*MP*, 302/*TP*, 247)

Anomic: from *anomie*, the condition in which standards of definition and practice lose their application or are placed in suspension—as in the underworld. Or, alternatively, it is a condition of aphasia in which the names of things are forgotten. "Anomalous" thus means that "becoming-animal" is something that itself cannot be terminated either by a limit or by language. "What is real is the becoming itself, the block of becoming, not the supposedly fixed terms through which that which becomes passes. Becoming can and should be qualified as becoming-animal even in the absence of a term that would be the animal become. The becoming-animal of the human being is real, even if the animal the human being becomes is not" (*MP*, 291/*TP*, 238). What is it, then?

From Body to Flesh

Perhaps we can gain some purchase on this question by way of Georges Bataille's conception of the *heterogeneous* as a form or element of existence that is sacred or accursed, that is, exterior with respect to the human order that it helps to establish (recall the *bare life* of the wolf-man):

> This consists of everything rejected by *homogeneous* society as waste or as superior transcendent value. Included are the waste products of the human body and certain analogous matter (trash, vermin, etc.); the parts of the body; persons, words, or acts having a suggestive erotic value; the various unconscious processes such as dreams or neuroses; the numerous elements or social forms that *homogeneous* society is powerless to assimilate: mobs, the warrior, aristocratic and impoverished classes, different types of violent individuals or at least those who refuse the rule (madmen, leaders, poets).[3]

Heterogeneity is whatever is decomposable: filth, excrement, the great unwashed; whatever contaminates or defiles—the *abject* or the sick; whatever is untouchable or unspeakable, like the homology of mouth and anus; above all, whatever one must not eat.[4]

(A corpse, for example. Julia Kristeva writes: "A wound with blood and pus, or the sickly, acrid smell of sweat, of decay, does not *signify* death. In the presence of signified death—a flat encephalograph, for instance—I would understand, react, accept. No, as in true theater, without makeup or masks, refuse and corpses *show me* what I permanently thrust aside in order to live. These bodily fluids, this defilement, this shit are what life withstands, hardly and with difficulty, on the part of death. There, I am at the border of my condition as a living being. My body extricates itself, as being alive, from that border. Such wastes drop so that I might live, until, from loss to loss, nothing remains in me and my entire body falls beyond the limit—*cadere*, cadaver.")[5]

For Bataille (following a certain reading of Hegel), *becoming human* is predicated upon the evacuation of the heterogeneous, which means the negation of nature, the prohibition or abjection of animal functions, and, indeed, the repression or exclusion of the entire ontology of the flesh: "Man is the animal that negates nature: he negates it through labor, which destroys it and changes it into an artificial world; he negates it in the case of life-creating activity; he negates it in the case of death. The incest prohibition is one of the effects of the repugnance felt for his condition by the animal that became human. The forms of animality were excluded from a bright world which signified humanity (*AS*, 61–62)."[6] Becoming human means the transformation of flesh into the *body of strength*, the heroic body that is impervious to whatever is not itself, above all impervious to suffering and (ignominious) death, including the experience of desire, hunger, pain, and fear; impervious, moreover, to the gaze of the other, whether human or animal.

The distinction between body (*corps*) and flesh (*chair*) is canonical.[7] *Body* is a Greek concept. It is what has been shaped into a thing of beauty and object of regard; it is self-possessed, which means under control and capable of struggle and achievement. Marble is its apotheosis. *Flesh* meanwhile is a biblical concept (*hasar* in Hebrew). It is essentially passive and weak, torpid and shapeless, wet and fragrant, warm and luxurious, yet for all that driven and hungry because insatiable (concupiscent). Flesh is for eating and being eaten, whereas the body is defined by self-denial or self-transcendence (one sinks into corpulence, whereas the body is fleet of foot, swift and agile like Achilles—whose heel, alas, is his one piece of flesh).[8] When the Greek hero enters the household (*oikos*), however, he enters a fleshly domain where he is perhaps more vulnerable than on the battlefield. Flesh is the natural site of suffering, punishment, and sacrifice—which in turn can be reinterpreted as events of becoming-human or human embodiment over which the spirit presides as if it were a priesthood whose dominion and authority and power are asserted by ascesis, celibacy, and cerebral solitude.[9] ("Every time desire is betrayed, cursed, uprooted from its field of immanence, a priest is behind it" [*MP*, 191/*TP*, 154].) The flesh, from the priestly point of view, must be overcome; otherwise it will consume itself. What interests Bataille, however, is the denial or reversal of this negation of nature: namely, an experience of consumption or nonproductive expenditure (*dépense*) that takes place in sacrificial meals, festivals of transgression, and various forms of eroticism in which the body is returned to the responsive/receptive condition of flesh.[10] The paradox of being human is that only human beings are capable of transgressing the boundaries that determine what they are; moreover, these transgressions are not (just) accidents—moments of weakness or failure of spirit—but in fact take the form of a festive return to nature, that is, to the border or originary scene of self-creation: "Since man has uprooted himself from nature, that being who returns to it is still uprooted, he is an uprooted being who suddenly goes back toward that from which he is uprooted, from which he has not ceased to uproot himself. The first uprooting is not obliterated: when men, in the course of the festival, give free play to the impulses they refuse in profane times, these impulses have a meaning in the context of the human world: they are meaningful only in that context. In any case, these impulses cannot be mistaken for those of animals" (*AS*, 90). Call these *impulses of the flesh*, or that which heeds the call of nature. (Here would be the place to return to Rabelais and his celebrations of eating, drinking, and defecation.)

The Body Without Organs

Flesh tends toward the faceless, featureless, structureless (perhaps that is the whole point of nature's call). Deleuze and Guattari's celebrated Body without Organs (BwO), the egg-like surface of random desires that resists organization, subjectification, and signification (socialization, for short), is a kind of archetype of the flesh—zones of sensation always in the state of becoming: "The body without organs is an egg: it is criss-crossed with axes and thresholds, with latitudes and longitudes and geodesic lines, traversed by *gradients* marking the transitions and the becomings, the destinations of the subject developing along these particular vectors. Nothing here is representative; rather it is all life and lived experience (*AO*, 19)."[11] In other words, a body without organs is not deficient; there is nothing lacking in it except the consent to be a proper organism, that is, the subject of stratification within a regime of signs:

> Let us consider the three great strata concerning us, in other words, the ones that most directly bind us: the organism, signifiance, and subjectification. The surface of the organism, the angle of signifiance and interpretation, and the point of subjectification or subjection. You will be organized, you will be an organism, you will articulate your body—otherwise you're just depraved. You will be a signifier and signified, interpreter and interpreted—otherwise you're a deviant. You will be a subject, nailed down as one, a subject of the enunciation recoiled into a subject of the statement, otherwise you're just a tramp. (*MP*, 197/*TP*, 159)

Depraved, deviant, derelict—in other words, abnormal (or, more accurately, anomalous); but imagine these as *practices* or molecular forms of life. In the chapter "How Do You Make Yourself a Body Without Organs?" *A Thousand Plateaus* gives us a recipe: "To the strata as a whole, the BwO opposes *disarticulation* (or *n* articulations) as the property of the plane of consistency, *experimentation* as the operation on that plane (no signifier, never interpret!), and *nomadism* as the movement (keep moving, even in place, never stop moving, motionless voyage desubjectification)" (*MP*, 197–98/*TP*, 159; my emphases). Above all, avoid all forms of incarceration.

The prototype of the BwO is Bataille's contemporary, Antonin Artaud, the theater visionary most famous perhaps for his drug addictions, schizophrenia, and the scatological ferocity of his later writings ("All writing is pigshit"), which are, among other things, polemical outbursts against psychiatrists and their techniques of normalization (most famously, shock treatments).

> If there had been no doctors
> there would never have been any sick people
> no dead skeletons
> sick people to be butchered and flayed
> for it was with doctors and not with sick people that society began. (*AA*, 529)

Artaud is Deleuze and Guattari's schizo-hero in their critique of Oedipal psychoanalysis and its affiliates (capitalism, systematic philosophy, structural linguistics, universal concepts, linear composition, regimes of normalcy of whatever kind). In the *Anti-Oedipus* we read: "Artaud makes a shambles of psychiatry, precisely because he is a schizophrenic and not because he is not. Artaud is the fulfillment of literature, precisely because he is a schizophrenic and not because he is not. It has been a long time since he broke down the wall of the signifier: Artaud the Schizo. From the depths of his suffering and his glory, he has the right to denounce what society makes of the psychotic" (*AO*, 35). Not that they counsel drugs, masochism, and paranoia—not exactly: the BwO, they protest, is "full of gaiety, ecstasy, and dance" (*MP*, 187/*TP*, 150)—but Artaud's bodily disarticulation (no less a real experience for being schizoid) is a synecdoche of Deleuze and Guattari's anarchism:

> What else?
> He is this unframed hole
> which life wanted to frame.
> because it's not a hole
> > but a nose
> that always knew too well how to sniff
> the wind of the apocalyptic
> > head
> which they stuck on his tight ass,
> and how good Artaud's ass is
> for the pimps in penitence. (*AA*, 528)

Interestingly, Deleuze and Guattari don't take up Artaud's "theater of cruelty," whose aim is not to stage cultural masterpieces but to make the audience experience its flesh in the form of fear, delirium, and limit-experiences of sensation.[12] One can see in Artaud the influence of Bataille. In one of his manifestos Artaud writes: "The theater cannot become itself again . . . until it provides the spectator with the truthful precipitates of dreams, in which his taste for crime, his erotic obsessions, his savagery, his fantasies, his utopian sense of life and of things, even his cannibalism, pour out on a level that is not counterfeit and illusory but internal" (*AA*, 244). But perhaps more interesting is the sheer physicality of Artaud's theater, where the mise-en-scène is not mere staging but becomes an attack on the spectator's senses: language is for screaming rather than for dialogue; traditional musical instruments will be replaced by "new alloys of metals [to] achieve a new diapason of the octave and produce intolerable ear-shattering sounds or noises" (*AA*, 247). And likewise new technologies of lighting equipment must be developed: "In view of the peculiar action of light on the mind, the effects of luminous vibrations must be investigated, along with new ways of diffusing light in waves, or sheets, or in fusillades of fiery arrows . . . with a view to producing heat, cold, anger, fear, etc." (*AA*, 247–48): a theater not of estrangement but of derangement.

Artaud was never able to put his theory of the theater into practice, but his ideas have had a wide-ranging afterlife. The modern rock concert, with its laser lights and heavy-metal acoustics, is one version of the theater of cruelty, but perhaps more emphatic would be some of the more radical forms of performance and body art, as when the Vienna Aktionists covered their naked bodies with the blood and entrails of slaughtered animals; or when Chris Burden had himself shot in the arm with a pistol, or placed in a sack on a busy street; or when the French performance artist Orlan had her face surgically removed—the surgery, meanwhile, being telecast via satellite to various points around the globe. As Parveen Adams describes it: "During her operation Orlan's face begins to detach itself from her head. We are shocked at the destruction of our normal narcissistic fantasy that the face 'represents' something. Gradually the 'face' becomes pure exteriority. It no longer projects the illusion of depth. It becomes a mask without any relation of representation. In turn this disturbs a fundamental illusion concerning the inside and the outside, that the outside provides a window onto what is represented. In this sense Orlan uses her head quite literally to demonstrate an axiom of at least one strand of feminist thought: *there is nothing behind the mask.*"[13] Appropriately, Orlan calls her aesthetic "carnal art," not "body art": an art of the *flesh* that, as she says, is much more painful to see than to create.[14]

Dismantle the Face

The face as removable flesh has an important place in Deleuze's thinking, as in his book on the artist Francis Bacon. In the chapter "The Body, the Meat, and the Spirit: Becoming Animal," Deleuze writes:

> As a portraitist, Bacon is a painter of heads, not faces, and there is a great difference between the two. For the face is a structured, spatial organization that conceals the head, whereas the head is dependent on the body, even if it is the point of the body, its culmination. It is not that the head lacks spirit; but it is a spirit in bodily form, a corporeal and vital breath, an animal spirit. It is the animal spirit of man: a pig-spirit, a buffalo-spirit, a dog-spirit, a bat-spirit.... Bacon thus pursues a very peculiar project as a portrait painter: *to dismantle the face*, to rediscover the head or make it emerge from beneath the face. (FB, 19)

Dismantle the face: without the face, the body becomes-animal, that is, becomes *flesh* or *meat*—something that loses definition as it is removed from its bones: "Meat is the state of the body in which flesh and bone confront each other locally rather than being composed structurally. The same is true of the mouth or teeth, which are little bones. In meat, the flesh seems to *descend* from the bones, while the bones rise up from the flesh" (FB, 20–21).

Arguably the mouth is what is most fleshly about us (Bataille thinks the *open* mouth is bestial, in contrast to "the narrow constipation of a strictly human attitude, the magisterial look of the face with a *closed* mouth" [VE, 60]).[15] This is certainly the case in Francis Bacon's work, where the mouth often consumes the face by opening as wide as possible in a grimace or scream—most famously in the *Study after Vélazquez's Portrait of Pope Innocent X* (1953), but perhaps most spectacularly in the earlier *Painting* (1946), which gives us a seated figure under an umbrella inside what looks to be a meat-locker in a butcher's shop ("I've always been very moved by pictures about slaughterhouses and meat," Bacon once said, "and to me they belong very much to the whole thing of the Crucifixion.... Of course, we are meat, we are potential carcasses. If I go into a butcher shop I always think it's surprising that I wasn't there instead of the animal").[16] All we see of the figure's head is its lower jaw, with its large wide mouth open to show a row of teeth above a fleshy lower lip—the upper lip appears to have been cut away so that all that remains is raw flesh. The painting is an *effacement* that leaves us with nothing but a mouth more monstrous than human. (Compare the mouths that appear at the end of long, reptilian necks in *Three Studies for Figures at the Base of a Crucifixion* [1944].)

Meanwhile Bacon reminds us that swelling is proper to the flesh, as in his *Study for Three Heads* (1962), and particularly his self-portraits where his own face loses definition in the manner of a pummeled prize-fighter. Deleuze's interest in this deformation or disappearance of the face can be traced back to the chapter on "Faciality" in *A Thousand Plateaus* in which Deleuze and Guattari propose what we might think of as a distinctively anti-Levinasian theory of the face. Whereas for Levinas the face-to-face relation, my exposure to the face of the other, is where my being-human is enacted in the form of responsibility for the other, for Deleuze and Guattari "the face is a horror story" (*MP*, 206/*TP*, 168). "The face is not an envelope exterior to the person who speaks, thinks, or feels" (*MP*, 205–6/*TP*, 167). It is something laid on from the outside that allows me to pass into human society but only within certain narrow corridors defined by the faciality of my face. The white European male face defines the apex from which humanity declines by degrees into the faces of women, children, non-Westerners, subalterns, aborigines, hominids, troglodytes, chimpanzees, pets, bats, flies.[17] Imagine having a face no one feels obliged to (or can bear to) regard—no eye-contact for you; perhaps one then resorts to surgery of the kind that Orlan parodies, especially when she has her face transformed into grotesque masks. In any case, the face is a regime of socialization to be escaped:

> The face is not animal, but neither is it human in general; there is even something absolutely inhuman about the face. It would be an error to proceed as though the face became inhuman only beyond a certain threshold: close-up,

extreme magnification, recondite expression, etc. *The inhuman in human beings: that is what the face is* [my emphasis]. It is by nature a close-up, with its animate white surfaces, its shining black holes, its emptiness and boredom. Bunkerface. To the point that if human beings have a destiny, it is rather to escape the face, to dismantle the face and facializations, to become imperceptible, to become clandestine, not by returning to animality, nor even by returning to the head, but by quite spiritual and special becoming-animal, by strange true becomings that get past the wall and get out of the black holes that make *faciality traits* themselves finally elude the organization of the face—freckles dashing toward the horizon, hair carried off by the wind, eyes you traverse instead of seeing yourself in or gazing in those glum face-to-face encounters between signifying subjectivities. (*MP*, 209/*TP*, 170–71)

Dismantle the face: this is precisely what Bacon's portraits accomplish, which is why Deleuze sees Bacon finally as something other than the pessimistic, nihilistic chronicler of twentieth-century horror that his name tag has come to represent. "If there is feeling in Bacon," he says, "it is not a taste for horror, it is pity, an intense pity: pity for flesh, including the flesh of dead animals" (*FB*, xxix).

(Meanwhile, in *The Open* Giorgio Agamben reminds us that Pico della Mirandola, in his famous oration on human beings, says that as created man is without form or feature, God having used up all available models: "He does not even have a face of his own (*nec proprium faciem*) and must shape it at his own discretion in either bestial or divine form" [*O*, 29].)

Non-Identity

For Deleuze and Guattari (who have, after all, read their Blanchot) non-identity is not a deprivation, not a negative, but a form of micropolitics whose structure is molecular, where non-identity is difference in itself unrelated to the bipolarity (the "bipolar machine") of identity/difference; hence it is very different from macro or identity politics whose structure is molar, where difference presupposes a prior identity—for example, man is a presupposition of woman: "All becomings are molecular: the animal, flower, or stone one becomes are molecular collectivities, haecceities, not molar subjects, objects, or forms that we know from the outside and recognize from experience, through science, or by habit" (*MP*, 337/*TP*, 275). Hence the paradox of "becoming-woman" that a number of feminists have struggled to resolve:[18]

> What we term a molar entity is, for example, the woman as defined by her form, endowed with organs and functions and assigned as a subject. Becoming-woman is not imitating this entity or even transforming oneself into it.... On the contrary, the woman as molar entity *has to become-woman* in order that the man also becomes- or can become-woman. It is, of course, indispensable for women to conduct a molar politics, with a view to winning back their own organism, their own history, their own subjectivity: "we as women . . . " makes its appearance as a subject of enunciation. But it is dangerous to confine oneself to such a subject, which does not function without drying up a spring or stopping a flow. (*MP*, 337–38/*TP*, 275–76)

As Stevie Schmiedel says: "*Becoming-woman* . . . is not to become woman, but to become molecular, polysemic, non-organic, or better, not defined by organs and their functions."[19] The idea is not to let "woman" become fixed as an *order-word*, the articulation of imperatives, notwithstanding, as Deleuze and Guattari indicate, the strategic necessity of banding together to unsettle the order of things.

Better to invent new concepts, like Donna Haraway's *cyborg*: "The cyborg is a creature in a post-gender world; it has no truck with bisexuality, pre-oedipal symbiosis, unalienated labor, or other seductions to organic wholeness through a final appropriation of all the powers of the parts into a higher unity" (*Simians, Cyborgs, and Women*, 150).[20] From a Deleuzean standpoint, a cyborg is a "line of flight" that escapes the segmentarity of molar organizations. It is not just a kind of entity (a hybrid) but a body without organs whose desires are mobile, unregulated, and (since they aren't provoked or defined by the *lack* of an object) capable of multiple forms of satisfaction—in other words, open to experiment. So not surprisingly the cyborg inhabits a "zone of indiscernibility" between human and animal, even to the point of rescuing bestiality from its long-standing residence as a taboo. In other words, nothing is forbidden. Another way to put this would be to say that the cyborg rescues animals from the "binary machine" that opposes them to human beings. So from a cyborg point of view, supposing there to be only one such thing, how we are with respect to animals is open not only to the invention of new concepts but also, following Ian Hacking's "dynamic nominalism," to *new ways to be*, not just for ourselves but for animals as well.[21]

This perhaps helps to explain or elaborate what Deleuze and Guattari might mean when they say that "becoming-animal" affects animals as well as humans. Consider the controversies over whether and/or in what sense animals can be considered "persons." Part of the problem is that animals are anomalies in the nature of the case. Elisa Aaltola writes: "Objectivity, and existing as oneself, are based on either *full personhood*, or *full materialism*, and it is the beings that fall in between that remain lacking of these qualities. This reveals the presumed nature of animals: they are 'in between' people and material things—animality is formed of 'in betweenness,' and hence lacks a permanent and independent quality."[22] So we really can't say what animals are, supposing that they are just one thing. Thinking of them as "persons" circumvents this dilemma by putting to one side the ontological question of "what" animals might be since they are neither humans nor things; likewise it displaces the question of what animals might "have" that would qualify them as persons. On what Aaltola plausibly takes to be the best account of personhood, persons are those who interact with one another: "Personhood is *experienced* rather than *conceptualized*," she says, and she cites an expert on primates as follows: "'Others are not understood as persons because we infer from their behaviour that they must have intentions and ideas about other people's intentions, but because we are capable of engaging with them in specific patterns of intersubjective interactions that include emotional and expressive behaviours. . . . Persons are capable of representing others as 'second persons,' i.e. as creatures capable of representing others as 'second persons,' i.e. as creatures capable of engaging in intersubjective encounters'" (191). It is a fact of experience that animals engage us, and we them, as "second persons." Empathy does not draw a line between animals and humans; or, as Aaltola puts it, "there is no categorical difference in the type of interaction we can have with other animals, and interactions with other humans" (19). And so she concludes (persuasively): "Animals should be *approached as persons* when considering whether or not they should be defined as persons" (20).

Naturally the question is whether we are up to the task. This question is nicely formulated in one of the fictional lectures that make up J. M. Coetzee's *The Lives of Animals*. In "The Philosophers and the Animals," an Australian novelist named Elizabeth Costello gives a lecture at a place called Appelton College on the human treatment of animals in which, having cited a famous essay by Thomas Nagel on "What Is It Like to Be a Bat?" she proposes that "there are no bounds to the sympathetic imagination": just as we can turn ourselves into a character in a novel and experience that character's experiences, so we can turn ourselves into any living thing, whether "a bat or a chimpanzee or an oyster."[23] Elizabeth Costello (or J. M. Coetzee) gives no examples of doing such a thing, but in responding to Coetzee's stories the ethnologist Barbara Smuts describes in detail her intersubjective relations with baboons and, later, gorillas during her sojourns in Africa. By her accounts it is no trouble for a human being to integrate him or herself into simian forms of life and to engage in personal relations with primates: "becoming-animal" seems a good way to put it. Here is her most telling anecdote:

> About thirty meters away, I came upon a "nursery" group of mothers and infants.... I sat near them and watched the mothers eating and the babies playing for timeless, peaceful moments. Then my eyes met the warm gaze of an adolescent female, Pandora. I continued to look at her, silently sending friendliness her way. Unexpectedly, she stood and moved closer. Stopping right in front of me, with her face at eye level, she leaned forward and pushed her large, flat, wrinkled nose against mine. I know that she was right up against me, because I distinctly remember her warm, sweet breath fogged up my glasses, blinding me. I felt no fear and continued to focus on the enormous affection and respect I felt for her. Perhaps she sensed my attitude, because in the next moment I felt

her impossibly long ape arms wrap around me, and for precious seconds, she held me in her embrace. Then she released me, gazed once more into my eyes, and returned to munching leaves. (114)

One wonders what Emmanuel Levinas would have made of this.

The more interesting question would concern Pandora's perspective: Whom did she see? Whom did she embrace? The question of "who?" needs the attention in the next chapter, because the "who" comes into play beneath the level of "what"—that is, beneath the level of categories and distinctions—where creatures are absolutely *singular*: irreducible, non-identical, and face-to-face with one another.

Derrida's Cat
(WHO AM I?)

> I would say that for me the great question is always the question *who*. Call it biographical, autobiographical or existential, the form of the question *who* is what matters to me, be it in, say, its Kierkegaardian, Nietzschean, or Heideggerian form. *Who? Who asks the question who? Where? How? When? Who arrives?* It is always the most difficult question, the irreducibility of *who* to *what*, or the place where between the *who* and *what* the limit trembles, in some way. It is clear that the *who* withdraws from or provokes the displacement of the categories in which biography, autobiography, and memoirs are thought.
> —Derrida, *A Taste for the Secret*

The Naked Animal

How exactly does Jacques Derrida address "the question *who*," and what does he make of it? This is what I would like to determine. In a characteristically exorbitant and playful text, "L'animal que donc je suis," the first of several lectures that he presented at a conference on the "autobiographical animal" held at Cérisy-la-Salle in 1997, Derrida tells of his discomfort when, emerging from the shower one day, he found himself being looked at by his cat.[1] What sort of event is this? We've been told what it is to be seen by someone else—this, says Sartre, is how we know there are other *subjects*, and it is also how we know what it is to be an object, which means feeling the debasement of being a mere thing. More precisely (for Sartre), it means that suddenly my consciousness, which so far had been intentional and unreflective—that is, of the world and of things in it—is now inhabited by a *self*. But becoming a *self*

79

in this way is, paradoxically, a form of alienation. Being seen by another, I fall out of the world that heretofore had been mine: "If there is an Other, whatever or whoever he may be, whatever may be his relations with me, and without his acting upon me in any way except by the pure upsurge of his being—then I have an outside, I have a *nature*. My original fall is the existence of the Other. Shame—like pride—is the apprehension of myself as a nature although that very nature escapes me and is unknowable as such" (*BN*, 352). So who am I?

This is the regulating question of "L'animal que donc je suis." The issue, as we shall see, is whether for Derrida the question "Who am I?" has (or should have) any sort of answer.

As Herman Rapaport has suggested, Derrida's experience of the gaze of his cat is a kind of parody of Sartre's story of the look:[2]

> I often ask myself, just to see, *who I am* [*qui je suis*]—and who I am (following) at the moment [*et qui je suis au moment*] when, caught naked, in silence, by the gaze of an animal, for example the eyes of a cat, I have trouble, yes, a bad time overcoming my embarrassment.
>
> Whence this malaise [*ce mal*]?
>
> I have trouble repressing a reflex dictated by immodesty. Trouble keeping silent within me a protest against the indecency. Against the impropriety that comes of finding oneself naked, one's sex exposed, stark naked before a cat that looks at you without moving, just to see. The impropriety [*malséance*] of a certain animal nude before the other animal, from that point on one might call it a kind of *animalséance*: the single, incomparable and original experience of the impropriety that would come from appearing in truth naked, in front of the insistent gaze of the animal, a benevolent or pitiless gaze, surprised or cognizant. The gaze of a seer, visionary, or extra-lucid blind person. It is as if I were ashamed, therefore, naked in front of this cat, but also ashamed for being ashamed. A reflected shame, the mirror of a shame ashamed of itself, a shame that is at the same time specular, unjustifiable, and unable to be admitted to. At the optical center of this reflection would appear this thing—and in my eyes the focus of this incomparable experience—that is called nudity. And about which it is believed that it is

proper to man, that is to say, foreign to the animals, naked as they are, or so it is thought, without the slightest inkling of being so. (*LAN*, 18/*ANT*, 3-4)

Derrida in this moment is caught by surprise—surprised, not just by his cat, but by his embarrassment, the unexpected shame of his nudity before the cat (as if the cat could care!). A human being, not wanting to embarrass a naked human being, would perhaps look away, pretending not to see; a lover, for whom nudity could have its attractions, might look him or her in the eye, or up and down. But what can a cat know—or, for all of that, what can we know? And so Derrida's sense of shame is doubled: imagine anyone, much less a philosopher (that sealed-off guardian of rationality), being embarrassed by a cat. *Who am I* at this moment? *Who am I* that I should experience myself (and my cat?) in this way?

Of course, what Derrida experiences is just his own flesh, being in the flesh, "naked as a beast [*bête*]" (*LAN*, 19/*ANT*, 4), but also *more* naked, since an animal cannot (or so we are told) experience its own animality or nudity: "In principle [but not in fact?], with the exception of man, no animal has ever thought to dress itself. Clothing would be proper to man, one of the 'properties' of man. 'Dressing oneself' would be inseparable from all the other forms of what is proper to man, even if one talks about it less than speech or reason, the *logos*, history, laughing, mourning, burial, the gift, and so on" (*LAN*, 19/*ANT*, 5). To which Derrida adds a parenthesis: "(The list of 'what is proper' to man always forms a configuration, from the first moment. For that very reason, it can never be limited to a single trait and it is never closed . . .)" (*LAN*, 19/*ANT*, 5). That is, there is no one thing that sets us apart from animals, unless perhaps it is our occasional *bestiality*, just as there is no such thing as the *animal as such*: this is one of Derrida's theses in this text—as it has been elsewhere, in different forms, as in the various elucidations of *différance*, where the idea is not so much to clarify (or obscure) differences as to diversify them. The many (you and me, for example) are others of each other, but not of any One.

To be sure: "There is no nudity 'in nature'" (*LAN*, 19/*ANT*, 5). There is flesh and the experience of flesh (cold, pain, hunger, desire) but not embarrassment or shame, that is (presumably), no experience of being naked. If so, of course, the joke is that if the cat had not looked at the naked Derrida, he (Derrida) would have remained (like) an animal, unaware of his nudity. The gaze of the cat is what makes him human—a point on which Derrida ruminates (and to which he will implicitly return in his reading of Genesis): "Before the cat that looks at me naked, would I be ashamed *like* a beast that no longer has the sense of its nudity? Or, on the contrary, *like* a man who retains the sense of his nudity? Who am I therefore? [*Qui suis-je alors?*] Who is it that I am (following)? [*Qui est-ce que je suis?*]" (*LAN*, 20/*ANT*, 5–6).

Who am I? What is the sense of this question? Derrida doesn't say (here), but for him, *the* "autobiographical animal," obsessed (as he confesses) with memory, "Who am I?" is perhaps *the* question of his philosophy or at all events of his elusive way of thinking—or of his elusive way of thinking of himself, as when he says, in *A Taste for the Secret*, "I am not one of the family": "'I am not one of the family' means: do not consider me 'one of you,' 'don't count me in,' I want to keep my freedom, always: this, for me, is the condition not only for being singular and other, but also for entering into relation with the singularity and alterity of others" (*TS*, 27).

The Other Cat (*l'autre absolu*)

Who am I (if I am not one of you, whoever you are)? Framed this way, it appears that, at the very least, the question *who* aims to overturn the rule of identity or the rule of the concept. Derrida's wide-ranging (digressive) reflections on his cat, on his relation with the animal-other, and on the way this relation alters his self-relation (including the whole business of being called "human," or of being an "I") are his way of allowing this question to do its unsettling work. For a start we should notice that Derrida asks pointedly about a *who*, not a *what*.[3] In the same spirit he says: "I must immediately make it clear that the cat I am talking about is a real cat, truly, believe me, a *little* cat. It isn't the *figure* of a cat. It doesn't silently enter the room as an allegory for all the cats on earth, the felines that traverse our myths and religions, literature and fables. There are so many of them. The cat I am talking about does not belong to Kafka's vast zoopoetics, something that nevertheless merits concern and attention here, endlessly and from a novel perspective" (*LAN*, 20/*ANT*, 6). No beast-fable homonizations. The cat in question is a *singular* cat, Derrida's cat, not a stand-in and interpreter from a philosopher's point of view, not a *literary* cat like one of Baudelaire's or Rilke's—although, by way of comparison or contrast, Rilke's famous "Schwarz Katze" would have been worth a moment's reflection. Recall how she lies there, indifferent to your look, until:

—auf einmal kehrt sie, wie geweckt,
ihr Gesicht und mitten in das deine:
und da triffst du deinen Blick im geelen
Amber ihrer runden Augenstein
unerwartet wieder: eingeschlossen
wie ein ausgestorbenes Insekt.

—all at once
as if awakened, she turns her face to yours;
and with a shock, you see yourself, tiny,
inside the golden amber of her eyeballs
suspended, like a prehistoric insect.[4]

But there is no metaphor in the *look* of Derrida's cat, no embodiment of sinister felinity. Derrida's cat, like the naked philosopher himself, is a *who*, not a *what*—one wonders why Derrida doesn't tell us his cat's name, but only that it is a *little* cat. At any rate they encounter one another at the level of the singular, not as man and animal but face-to-face.

But can one's cat (any cat) really enter into such a relation? This seems to be the brunt of Derrida's question (and perhaps one of the central issues in his text): "How can an animal look you in the face?" (*LAN*, 24/*ANT*, 7). After all, according to psychoanalytic theory, an animal cannot even look itself in the face, since when it looks in a mirror (presumably we know this from experience) there is no experience of recognition, which is to say no formation of a subject.[5] Likewise Heidegger, in *What Is Called Thinking?* says: "Man is the animal that confronts face-to-face. A mere animal, such as a dog, never confronts anything, it can never confront anything *to its face*; to do so, the animal would have to perceive *itself.*"⁶ As if, like Dracula, an animal were invisible to mirrors. The orthodox thesis is, as Derrida says, that the animal is able to *react*, but not to *respond*, to what it sees. But it is just this thesis that, by way of the "unsubstitutable singularity" of his cat (*LAN*, 26/*ANT*, 9), Derrida wants to contest, and he does so by mapping onto his cat-encounter (something like) the ethical relation described by Emmanuel Levinas (I say, *something like*, because, as Matthew Calarco reminds us, Levinas doesn't really think animals have faces, either).⁷

No doubt, says Derrida, I am in advance of my cat, following it on the scale of creation or evolution, superior to it in every respect (except perhaps its imperturbability), but here and now my relation to this cat is one of *proximity*, which is what the term "face-to-face" means: not an objective relation of cognition and representation, but a relation of touching and being touched, a relation of responsiveness and responsibility, which for Levinas is very much a relation of skin-to-skin. So one can say that Derrida, standing there naked, is in a Levinasian (that is, accusative) situation vis-à-vis his cat. As he says, "[My cat] can look at me. It has its point of view regarding me. The point of view of the absolute other, and nothing will have ever given me more food for thinking through this absolute alterity of the neighbor or of the next(-door) than these moments when I see myself seen naked under the gaze of a cat" (*LAN*, 28/*ANT*, 11). Derrida's cat is an other like no other: *l'autre absolu*—transcendent with respect to his (Derrida's) superior powers of speech and reason, and above all imposing on Derrida a philosophical and perhaps even ethical demand ("nothing will have ever given me more food for thinking . . . "). Interestingly, Derrida does not introduce the term *Autrui* to identify his cat, but he does ascribe to the cat "a point of view," which means that between himself and his cat there is a reversal of subjectivity in which Derrida is no longer himself (that is, no longer self-possessed, able to say "I" without *malséance*).

But how can a cat be an *other*? Levinas says that "it is only man who could be absolutely foreign to me—refractory to every typology, to every genus, to every characterology, to every classification" (*TeI*, 71/*TI*, 73). To which Blanchot responded by saying that, if this is what "alterity" means (namely, outside every horizon), then "the Other man who is *'autrui'* also risks being always Other than man, close to what cannot be close to me: close to death, close to the night, and certainly as repulsive as anything that comes to me from these regions without a horizon" (*EI*, 103/*IC*, 72). In "And Say the Animal Responded?" Derrida sides with Blanchot by proposing the hypothesis of the "animal-*other*" in order to locate "a place of alterity that is radical enough to break with every identification of an image of self, with every fellow living creature, and so with every fraternity or human proximity, with all humanity" (*LAN*, 181/*ANT*, 132). We are always on the plane of resemblance with respect to other human beings. For Derrida the animal-*other* alone who compels the question, "Who am I?" What response is there to this question? Or, more exactly, what meaning or consequence does Derrida's response entail?

The "Abyssal Limit" of the Human

Of course, on Levinas's theory, the alterity of Derrida's cat entails his responsibility for it, that is, his responsibility for the good of his cat (who no doubt just wants to be let out), but also his ability to respond to it as in fact he *does* respond when he experiences his nakedness in his cat's (unfathomable) eyes. This is not an experience of himself as a subject, a *cogito*; it is an experience of his passivity (his flesh), which Derrida immediately names or renames *"the passion of the animal"*: "seeing oneself seen naked under a gaze behind which there is a bottomlessness, at the same time innocent and cruel perhaps, perhaps sensitive and impassive, good and bad, uninterpretable, unreadable, undecidable, abyssal and secret" (*LAN*, 29/*ANT*, 12). In which case Derrida's experience is not just an ethical event in Levinas's sense but is also, at the same time, what Maurice Blanchot (following Georges Bataille) calls a "limit-experience," that is, an experience of utter passivity, as in an experience of fatigue, waiting, affliction, dying, but also of the passivity of the child).[8] Here is how Derrida describes it:

> As with every bottomless gaze, as with the eyes of the other, the gaze called "animal" offers to my sight the abyssal limit of the human: the inhuman or the ahuman, the ends of man, that is to say the bordercrossing from which vantage

man dares to announce himself to himself, thereby calling himself by the name that he believes he gives himself. And in these moments of nakedness, under the gaze of the animal, everything can happen to me, I am like a child ready for the apocalypse, *I am (following) the apocalypse itself* [*je suis l'apocalypse même*], that is to say the ultimate and first event of the end, the unveiling and the verdict (*LAN*, 31/*ANT*, 12).

So here we are again at a border crossing: the anomalous space-between in which no one is anything, neither human nor nonhuman but inhuman or ahuman—perhaps one could also say "prehuman" or (as many now say) "posthuman": anyway, without horizons or signposts of any kind. Recall Giorgio Agamben's region of "bare life," the "zone of indistinction," in which no one is anything (*HS*, 104–11). The border is in any case aporetic, a limit that leaves him (Derrida) like a child before the brink, "ready for the apocalypse," or whatever is to come, rather like Bataille's ecstatic child in *Inner Experience*, left alone at night, "naked in the depths of the woods," enjoying or suffering an ecstasy of anguish; or like Blanchot's child in *The Writing of the Disaster*, exposed to the "primal scene" of an absolute exteriority that fills him with "devastation and joy," leaving him henceforward "to live withdrawn from any interest in [him]self, disinterested, thinned out to a state of utter calmness, expecting nothing" (in short, a kind of Blanchot).[9]

The presence of the child at these extreme limits is worth some attention. The child, like the animal, is a figure of bare life, inevitably invisible behind the well-fed subject of *enunciation* whom philosophers christen "Man as such." Meanwhile, for Agamben infancy is the "Ur-limit" of language, that is, the source or condition of its possibility insofar as it is a pure experience of language (an *experimentum linguae*), that is, not a *use* of language but a submersion in the materiality that makes voice (and, indeed, writing) possible (*IH*, 4–7). The infant is, like the animal, *within* language (*langue*) but on the hither side of speech (*parole*), in the semiotic or protosemantic world of babble (or Babel):

> It is not language in general that marks out the human form from other living beings—according to the Western metaphysical tradition that sees man as

a *zoon lógon échon* (an animal endowed with speech)—but the split between language and speech, between semiotic and semantic (in Benveniste's sense), between sign system and discourse. Animals are not in fact denied language; on the contrary, they are always and totally language. In them *la voix sacrée de la terre ingénue* (the sacred voice of the unknowing earth)—which Mallarmé, hearing the chirp of a cricket, sets against the human voice as *une* and *nondécomposée* (one and indivisible)—knows no breaks or interruptions. Animals do not enter language, they are already inside it. Man, instead, by having an infancy, by preceding speech, splits this single language and, in order to speak, has to constitute himself as the subject of language—he has to say *I*. Thus, if language is truly man's nature . . . then man's nature is split at its source, for infancy brings it discontinuity and the difference between language and discourse (*IH*, 59).[10]

So, on this theory, Derrida's cat is not without language (its sounds and voices) but, like the child, it splits the difference between the brute materiality of language and the intentionality of speech—and in the bargain it restores the *nondiscursive* region of language that philosophers of Derrida's generation were anxious to explore, often in the name of poetry or literature, as well as by way of their own baroque experiments in writing.[11]

Perhaps no one's writing is as baroque as Derrida's, which has never proceeded in a straightforward manner but unpredictably through amplifications and digressions punctuated by puns and neologisms. Arguably, this "style" is not just obscurantism but a protosemantic exploration of language beyond the limits of the propositional style of discursive reason. In his interview with Jean-Luc Nancy, "'Eating Well,'" Derrida writes:

> If one defines language in such a way that it is reserved for man, what is there to say? But if one reinscribes language in a network of possibilities that do not merely encompass it but mark it irreducibly from the inside, everything changes. I am thinking in particular of the mark in general, of the trace, of iterability, of *différance*. These possibilities or necessities, without which there would be no language, *are themselves not only human*. It is not a question of

covering up ruptures and heterogeneities. I would simply contest that they give rise to a single, linear, indivisible, oppositional limit, to a binary opposition between the human and the infrahuman. And what I am proposing here should allow us to take into account scientific information about the complexity of "animal languages," genetic coding, all forms of marking within which so-called human language, as original as it might be, does not allow us to "cut" once and for all where we would in general like to cut. As you can see, in spite of appearances, I am speaking here of very "concrete" and very "current" problems: the ethics and the politics of the living." (WC, 116–17)

In other words, one cannot appeal (as, for example, Heidegger does) to language as that which distinguishes us (*zōon logon echon*) from other living creatures (*alogon*). There is no one thing that can be called language, nor any one thing that can be called speech—which means no one thing of which animals, for example, can be said to be deprived, or humans endowed: no one line, in other words, that can separate ourselves from the other.[12]

L'Animot

Regarding the rule of the concept, we should take care not to miss the critical intervention Derrida undertakes in "L'animal que donc je suis." His complaint here is that philosophers and poets have traditionally engaged animals dogmatically by way of appellations from above rather than on the basis of ethological evidence that comes from *being with* animals in an extended and systematic way.[13] Already in Genesis the aboriginal encounter with other living things gets covered over or elided by a narrative of naming, which is itself aporetic, however, since it is (as Derrida reads it) about the contingency of a God who allows man to name the animals simply "in order to see" what he will call them, what names will be chosen, as if the genesis of being and time were a kind of animal experiment (*LAN*, 35–36/*ANT*, 17). Derrida writes: "This powerful yet deprived 'in order to see' that is God's, the first stroke of time, before time, God's exposure to surprise, to the event of what is going to occur between man and animal, this time before time has always made me dizzy" (*LAN*, 36/*ANT*, 17). As does the gaze of his cat.

What would it be for man and animal to encounter one another on the hither side of speech, as if before the naming of the animal and all that this has implied in terms of the long-sanctioned, unquestioned subjection of animals to human authority and control? Perhaps this is the import of Derrida's encounter with his cat. At any rate, for Derrida, the question of *being with* animals is not just hypothetical, given the fate of "the animal" since the beginnings of modernity, with its unprecedented "reduction of the animal not only to the production and overactive reproduction (hormones, genetic crossbreeding, cloning, and so on) of meat for consumption but also of all sorts of other end products, and all of that in the service of a certain being and the putative well-being of man" (*LAN*, 46/*ANT*, 25). Like Coetzee's Elizabeth Costello, Derrida does not hesitate to speak of genocide: "No one can deny seriously any more, or for very long, that men do all they can in order to dissimulate this cruelty or hide it from themselves, in order to organize on a global scale the forgetting or misunderstanding of this violence that some would compare to the worst cases of genocide (there are also animal genocides: the number of species endangered because of man takes one's breath away)" (*LAN*, 46/*ANT*, 25–26). Here is the context in which to cite, as Derrida does, Jeremy Bentham's famous line: the question of the animal is not whether it can think or speak but whether it can *suffer* (*LAN*, 50/*ANT*, 27).

It is, Derrida says, in the context of this subjection of the animal to the violence of modernity that we need to consider (or maybe discover for the first time) *the animal that looks at us* (and so makes a claim on us). In part this means starting philosophy (or even Genesis) all over again, rethinking how we figure the border that separates us from other living creatures, which means inventing new words to use when we speak about animals, not to say how we comport ourselves with respect to them.

Here perhaps is where many will grow impatient with Derrida, who seems more interested in how to think than in how to act. For example, in contrast to so many animal rights activists, Derrida's idea is not to erase the line that separates us from other living things (as if there were no such things as *differences*) but rather to multiply its dimensions—"*Limitrophy* is therefore my subject"

(*LAN*, 51/*ANT*, 29): literally, the *hypertrophy* or *pluralization* of limits, as well as of the creatures that are contained in them. The question of the animal, Derrida says, "becomes interesting once, instead of asking whether or not there is a limit that produces a discontinuity, one attempts to think what a limit becomes once it is abyssal, once the frontier no longer forms a single indivisible line but more than one internally divided line, once, as a result, it can no longer be traced, objectified, or counted as single and indivisible" (*LAN*, 52–53/ *ANT*, 30–31). The border is not fixed; it is not formal or logical. Above all, it is not generic but historical and variable and therefore open to exploration and experimentation, which is basically what the word "abyssal" implies.

And this means, first of all (for Derrida at any rate), breaking with the word "Animal," that is, breaking with the philosophical tradition from Aristotle to Lacan that speaks of the animal in general as a category meant to include "*all* that man does not recognize as his fellows, his neighbors, or his brothers" (*LAN*, 56/*ANT*, 34). As a way of crossing out the "Animal" (the way he had once crossed out "Being," which is what he has always wanted to do with "Man") Derrida coins the term *l'animot* (with its pun on *l'animaux*)—"a chimerical word that sounded as though it contravened the laws of the French language" (*LAN*, 65/*ANT*, 41). In the spirit of this neologism Derrida refers us to his "zootobiography," recalling all the many and varied animals that have appeared in his writings, including the lowly silkworm ("I . . . admit to my old obsession with a personal and somewhat paradisaic bestiary. It came to the fore very early on: the crazy project of constituting everything I have thought or written within a zoosphere, the dream of an absolute hospitality and an infinite appropriation. How to welcome or liberate so many animal-words (*animots*) *chez moi*?" [*LAN*, 60/*ANT*, 37]).[14] Derrida's work is nothing if not *chimerical* in the multiplicity of its animals, and this multiplicity—this invocation of a *philosophical bestiary* to replace a general category—is one of the principal tasks of his address:[15]

> [It] is a matter of taking into account a multiplicity of heterogeneous structures and limits. Among nonhumans, and separate from nonhumans, there is an immense multiplicity of other living things that cannot in any way be

homogenized, except by means of violence and willful ignorance, within the category of the animal or animality in general. From the outset there are animals and, let's say, *l'animot*. The confusion of all nonhuman living creatures within the general and common category of the animal is not simply a sin against rigorous thinking, vigilance, lucidity, or empirical authority; it is also a crime. Not a crime against animality precisely, but a crime of the first order against the animals, against animals. (*LAN*, 73/*ANT*, 48)

A "multiplicity of structures and limits": recall that in "The Ends of Man" Derrida says that, when it comes to *man*, "one must speak several languages and produce several texts at once."[16] The same principle holds when it comes to animals. What Derrida wants is an approach that would preserve the animal-*other* from its incorporation into an anthropocentric homogeneity, but even more particularly, one that would protect it from a reduction to the "animal machine" that Descartes constructed and which continues to inhabit (or to operate in) the writings of Kant and Heidegger, Levinas and Lacan, for each of whom the animal (in general) is consistently defined by its *incapacities*—its inability to do what humans do (speak, reason, mourn, laugh, cry, deceive). The animal, Lacan says, can react (like a computer) but not respond (as a subject). But what does it mean to respond?

Here it is worth noticing how Derrida differs from Martha Nussbaum and her "capabilities approach" to the question of the animal. Aristotle had argued that human beings are endowed with capacities that should be allowed to flourish; it is wrong to prevent people from living lives of which they are capable. The same principle, Nussbaum argues, should be applied to animals: "If [like Aristotle] we feel wonder looking at a complex organism, that wonder at least suggests the idea that it is good for that being to flourish as the kind of thing it is. And this idea is next door to the ethical judgment that it is wrong when the flourishing of a creature is blocked by the harmful agency of another."[17]

But this leaves open the question of how we are with these creatures. In her essay "Eating Meat and Eating People," the philosopher Cora Diamond wonders whether it is enough to figure our relations with other living things in terms of their capacities, whether for suffering or flourishing. Instead, she asks (in a way that seems symmetrical with Derrida's inquiry) what it is for us to single out living things as "fellow creatures." A "fellow creature," Diamond emphasizes, is not a biological concept, that is, it cannot be clarified by appealing to *what* a creature is or how it resembles or differs from us, but only by attending to the multifarious ways in which we interact with other creatures, human and otherwise, in our various forms of life.[18] Feeding birds and squirrels is a recognition of birds and squirrels as fellow creatures; the fattening of turkeys is another matter. The deer hunter who gives his quarry a sporting chance rather than simply trapping or poisoning it like a mouse relates to it as a fellow creature, whatever we may think about hunting. The complexity of the relation appears when we realize that, like the hunter (as opposed to the pest exterminator), we *do* frequently eat our fellow creatures, although we usually do not eat those with whom we live as companions, which is perhaps also the reason we do not, except perhaps under ritual (or desperate) circumstances, eat other people. A cow is for eating in a way that a pet dog is not, even as a calf raised by a member of a 4H club is a different creature from the calf in the stockyard, however biologically the same they may well be. Whatever its ultimate fate, a calf is not regarded as something to eat when it is addressed by name. It seems to me that Derrida is trying to get at this sort of plurality and complexity of differences (differences inaccessible to concepts and categories) when he rejects the idea that we are separated from "the animal" by "a single, indivisible, linear, oppositional limit." In fact, we are most concretely joined to animals on occasions that defeat our concepts—occasions in which animals are most uniquely themselves, like Derrida's "unsubstitutable cat." And this brings us back to our regulating question.

"Who?"

At one point in "L'animal que donc je suis," Derrida recalls the anecdote of the dog in Emmanuel Levinas's *Difficult Freedom*. One of the essays in this volume concerns the dogs that appear in various texts of Exodus, particularly 11:7 in which the dogs of Egypt, "with neither ethics nor *logos*," refuse to growl or bark, and so permit the escape of the Israelites from slavery.[19] As a gloss on this text, Levinas remembers his time in a prisoner-of-war camp during World War II:

> There were seventy of us in a forestry commando unit for Jewish prisoners of war in Nazi Germany. An extraordinary coincidence was the fact that the camp bore the number 1492, the year of the expulsion of Jews from Spain under the Catholic Ferdinand V. The French uniform still protected us from Hitlerian violence. But the other men, called free, who had dealings with us or gave us work or orders or even a smile—and the children and women who passed by and sometimes raised their eyes—stripped us of our human skin. We were subhuman, a gang of apes. A small inner murmur, the strength and wretchedness of persecuted people, reminded us of our essence as thinking creatures, but we were no longer part of the world. Our comings and goings, our sorrow and laughter, illnesses and distractions, the work of our hands and the anguish of our eyes, the letters we received from France and those accepted for our families—all that passed in parentheses. We were beings entrapped in their species, despite all their vocabulary, beings without language. Racism is not a biological concept; anti-Semitism is the archetype of all internment. Social aggression, itself, merely imitates this model. It shuts people away in a class, deprives them of expression and condemns them to being "signifiers without a signified" and from there to violence and fighting. How can we deliver a message about our humanity which, from behind the bars of quotation marks, will come across as anything other than monkey talk?
>
> And then, about halfway through our long captivity, for a few short weeks before sentinels chased him away, a wandering dog entered our lives. One day he came to meet this rabble as we returned under guard from work. He survived in some wild patch in the region of the camp. But we called him Bobby, an exotic name, as one does with a cherished dog. He would appear at morning assembly and was waiting for us as we returned, jumping up and down and barking with delight. For him, there was no doubt that we were human. (*DF*, 15–53)

How could one distinguish between *reaction* and *response* in Bobby's barking? What Derrida likes about this anecdote is that it subverts the fact that

Levinas describes Bobby in terms of his deprivations (*LAN*, 159–60/*ANT*, 107–108). "This dog was," Levinas says, "the last Kantian in Nazi Germany, without the brain needed to universalize maxims and drives" (*DF*, 153), that is, someone who, not knowing any better, is ethical in spite of himself (let's say "himself," since he's been given a proper name). But on what could one base this judgment of the shortfall of Bobby's brain, his lack of "ethics and *logos*," especially since, after all, the point of the anecdote is to make Bobby more responsive, more *humane*, and more ethical if not more human, than the nearby population for whom the prisoners are only so many apes?

Here is the problem Derrida wants us to consider:

> It is not just a matter of asking whether one has the right to refuse the animal such and such a power (speech, reason, experience of death, mourning, culture, institution, technics, clothing, lying, pretense of pretense, covering of tracks, gift, laughter, tears, respect, etc.—the list is necessarily without limit, and the most powerful philosophical tradition within which we live has refused the "animal" *all of that*). It *also* means asking whether what calls itself human has the right to rigorously attribute to man, which means therefore to attribute to himself, what he refuses the animal, and whether he can ever possess the *pure, rigorous, indivisible* concept, as such, of that attribution. (*LAN*, 185–86/*ANT*, 135)

In other words, Levinas's anecdote of the dog, like Derrida's story of his cat, raises the question, not of "the animal," but of *who I am* that refuses the animal-*other*. Who am *I* to attribute abilities to myself that I refuse to the animal-*other*? Indeed, by what right, that is, on what basis do I attribute to myself this or that capacity at all, whether I deny it to others or not? Can I give a philosophical account—develop a *"pure, rigorous, indivisible* concept"—of *any* of the capabilities, strengths, virtues, or distinctively human features that I confer upon myself? (Can I say what *man* is?) Here, of course, we recognize the Derrida who spent his philosophical career questioning and often satirizing the very idea of "pure, rigorous, indivisible" concepts, categories, distinctions, or substances of any kind. How else did he become (as, indeed, he posthumously remains) the Beelzebub that visits analytic philosophers whenever they hear his name?

But, more to the point at hand, what finally *is* the sense of the question "Who am I?"? Recall Blanchot on *"the unknown and slippery being of an indefinite 'Who?'"* (F, 291). The *who* is, after all, an *interrogative* pronoun: it presupposes the absence of definition. "Who is it?" "Who are you?" "Who goes there?" "Who comes after the subject?" "Who, me?" In contrast to the "givenness" of the "I" (the indubitably intrepid *cogito*), the mode of existence of the *who* is just that of being in doubt or in question, being addressed, accused, or called to account. The *who* is at the farthest remove from the grammar and context of the assertion, except perhaps to call it into question (*Who says that animals have no language?*). Likewise, in contrast to the "I," the *who* is precisely what cannot be conceptualized, that is, made the subject of a theory of the subject. The *who* is the elusive quarry of autobiography (a genre of inquiry), as if what were *conceptually* irreducible (without identity: I = I) could be captured in a narrative (although in practice mostly under a type: here is what I am like). For Derrida, however, the *who* belongs to the order of events at the level of the singular—as, for example, in the exposure of his naked flesh to the inscrutable gaze of his "unsubstitutable cat." The *who* is the unknown, the fugitive figure (as in the genre of the *whodunit*, except without promise of resolution). Dumb or stuttering is how I am apt to be struck by the question "Who are you?" There is no ready answer. A response would have to be improvised to fit the circumstances of the demand, not to mention the various emphases and implications that each word of the demand can support: "Who are you?" "Who are you, anyway?" "Who do you think you are?" It is not surprising that the question "who?" is frequently charged with impatience or even hostility. Not for nothing, Blanchot thought that being forced to speak—to answer—is worse than being kept silent (*EI*, 60/*IC*, 42–43, on the relation of speech and torture).

Likewise, in *A Taste for the Secret* Derrida affirms the absolute right not to answer, which is perhaps related to the law of hospitality, which holds that the stranger who arrives at your door is not to be treated with hostility but is to be welcomed without having to meet any conditions of identity—in other words, without having to answer "Who are you?" (*TS*, 26–27; compare Derrida, "Passions," *ON*, 17). Under conditions of hospitality, the deficiency of the *who* does not have to be made up, perhaps not even by the confession of one's proper name.[20] For Derrida this deficiency should not and, indeed, cannot be made up in any case (this seems to be the gist of the epigraph to this chapter: "It is clear that the *who* withdraws from or provokes the displacement of the categories in which biography, autobiography, and memoirs are thought"). To the question "Who am I?" there is no answer, for the simple reason that I am as much an other to myself as I am to my neighbor or to my host or, for that matter, to my cat. This in fact seems to be the regulating theme of Derrida's autobiographical writings, *Circonfession* and *Monolinguism of the Other*, which concern his own precarious or disordered identity as an Algerian Jew, or Franco-Maghrebian, whose love of the French language cannot conceal the fact that French is not his language, that he has no language, and that he is therefore in no position to say "I," except perhaps by way of a complex evasion that would be impossible for anyone to follow:

> If, for example, I dream of writing an anamnesis of what enabled me to identify myself or say *I* from the depths of amnesia and aphasia, I know, by the same token, that I can do it only by opening up an impossible path, leaving the road, escaping, giving myself the slip, inventing a language different enough to disallow its own *reappropriation* within the norms, the body, and the law of the given language—or by all the normative schemas constituted by programs of a grammar, a lexicon, a semantics, a rhetoric, speech genres or literary forms, stereotypes or cultural clichés (the most authoritarian of which remain mechanisms of avant-gardist reproducibility, and the indefatigable regeneration of the literary superego).[21]

"Who am I?" Derrida asks himself this question in the face of his cat, "just to see" if there might be an answer—or, more accurately, "just to see" what might come of it, for the question "who?" does not so much ask for an answer as propose the itinerary of an "impossible path," an escape ("giving oneself the slip") that would avoid absorption into an identity-machine, and so perhaps relieve that original *malséance* of his self-relation (an amnesia of a kind) provoked by the eyes or the mirror of his cat.

A final word on giving oneself the slip: the deficiency of the *who* is not a negative—not a deprivation but a kind of privacy that it is always criminal to invade or expose to view and whose preferred figure of speech would be the circumlocution (*circonfession*). Imagine the *who* as a singularity that cannot be captured by "the norms, the body, and the law of a given," including that of the signature, whose proper name is an appropriation of the sort that Derrida wants precisely to elude. Derrida has always inhabited Maurice Blanchot's neighborhood, where anonymity and discretion allow one to keep one's distance (that is, maintain one's freedom). In any event, whether in search or in flight, one is always "after" the *who*, including no doubt the *who* of one's cat. One can perhaps understand now why Derrida did not tell us his cat's name.

Notes

Prologue

1. Blanchot is thinking principally of Kafka, who, Blanchot says, kept a journal to remind himself "who he is when he isn't writing" (*EL*, 24/*SL*, 29), and of Mallarmé, for whom "the poetic word is no longer someone's word. In it no one speaks, and what speaks is not anyone" (*EL*, 42/*SL*, 41).
2. Blanchot, *L'entretien infini*, 94 / *The Infinite Conversation*, 67.
3. Blanchot, *Le pas au-delà*, 12 / *The Step Not Beyond*, 4.
4. Blanchot, *L'écriture du désastre*, 34 / *The Writing of the Disaster*, 18.
5. In *Totality and Infinity*, Levinas describes the ethical relation as a relation with another who is entirely outside my grasp and who interrupts my self-relation: "The absolutely other [*autre*] is the Other [*Autrui*]. He and I do not form a number.... Neither possession nor the unity of number nor the unity of concepts link me to the Stranger [*l'Étranger*], the Stranger who disturbs the being at home with oneself [*le chez soi*]. But Stranger also means the free one. Over him I have no power" (*TeI*, 28/*TI*, 39).
6. Levinas, *Autrement qu'être*, 194–205 / *Otherwise Than Being*, 121–28.
7. See Georges Bataille's essay on the "me" (*moi*), "Sacrifices," in *Visions of Excess*, 130–36. The "me" is very different from the Cartesian *ego* because of its absolute contingency and irreproducibility: "the very essence of the *me* consists in the fact that no other conceivable existence can replace it; the total improbability of my coming into the world poses, in an imperative mode, a total heterogeneity" (130). The *me* is not an "I" that exists (the first person singular is a mere abstraction, interchangeable with any other); on the contrary: "The *me* accedes to its specificity and to its integral transcendence only in the form of the '*me* that dies'" (132).
8. Nancy, *Tombe de sommeil*, 20 / *Fall of Sleep*, 5–6.
9. Nancy, *The Birth to Presence*, 13. The essay first appeared in Borch-Jacobsen, Michaud, and Nancy, *Hypnoses*.
10. Nancy begins his essay with a citation from Hegel: "'Identity, as self-consciousness, is what distinguishes man from nature, particularly from the brutes, which never reach the point of comprehending themselves as 'I,' that is, pure self-contained unity'" (*BP*, 9).
11. Nancy, *L'expérience de la liberté*. Here is Nancy's version of *finite freedom*: "The transcendence that makes freedom is the transcendence of finitude, since the essence of finitude is to not contain in itself its own essence" (*ExL*, 111/*EF*, 83).

12. This *finite* or, indeed, anarchic thinking of freedom can be traced back to Heidegger's critique of the violence of propositional thinking, as in the section on "Thing and Work" in "The Origin of the Work of Art," where he speaks of the resistance of mere things to the concepts with which we try to take hold of them: "This exertion of thought seems to meet with its greatest resistance in defining the thingness of the thing; for where else could the cause lie of the failure of the efforts mentioned? The unpretentious thing evades thought most stubbornly. Or can it be that this self-refusal of the mere thing, this self-contained independence, belongs precisely to the nature of the thing?" (Heidegger, *Poetry, Language, Thought,* 31–32). Later Heidegger introduced the phrase *Gelassenheit zu den Dingen* ("releasement toward things") to suggest a new comportment toward the world, an openness or responsibility toward things as against grasping them by means of concepts (interestingly, a German word for concept, *der Begriff,* derives from *greifen,* to grasp). See Heidegger, *Discourse on Thinking,* 56–57. See also Dallmayr, "The Ontology of Freedom," esp. 115–16.

13. The singular (singularity) is crucial to Nancy's thinking, but it is also a major preoccupation in French thinking from Bataille and Blanchot to the present. The singular is an existent outside the alternatives of universal and particular; it is more event than substance, an instance of diversity or alterity (and so there is no such thing as a single singularity). Levinas's *Autrui* is singular in this sense, as is the ethical subject who is responsible for the good of the other, come what may. For Gilles Deleuze, it is difference in itself, outside the alternatives of sameness and difference—see *Difference and Repetition,* passim. See also Nancy's essay "Someone" in *The Sense of the World,* 68–75.

14. Adorno, "Vers une musique informelle," 322. See also Adorno, *Aesthetic Theory,* 7: "For no single select category, not even the aesthetically central concept of the law of form, names the essence of art and suffices to judge its products. Essential to art are defining characteristics that contradict its fixed art-philosophical concept." Much of *Aesthetic Theory* is an attempt to come to terms with "aesthetic nominalism," or the resistance of the artwork to universals of any sort: "By pursuing its own identity with itself"—that is, its incomparability or singularity—"art assimilates itself with the nonidentical" (134).

15. Nancy, *L'oubli de la philosophie,* 84. In *The Inoperative Community* Nancy writes: "We" are not individuals but singularities, and "singularity never has the structure of individuality. Singularity never takes place at the level of atoms, those identifiable if not identical entities; rather, it takes place at the level of the *clinamen,* which is unidentifiable" (*CD,* 23–24/*InC,* 6–7). But later on Nancy puts it in more complicated terms: "We are alike because each one of us is exposed to the outside that we are *for ourselves.* The like is not the same [*le semblable n'est pas le pareil*]. I do not rediscover *myself,* nor do I recognize *myself* in the other: I experience the other's alterity, or I experience alterity in the other together with the alteration that 'in me' sets my singularity outside me and infinitely delimits it." To which, however, Nancy then adds, a bit incoherently:

"Community is that singular ontological order in which the other and the same are alike [sont le semblable]: that is to say, in the sharing of identity" (CD, 83–84/InC, 33–34).

16. Nancy, *Être singulier pluriel*, 48–54 / *Being Singular Plural*, 28–34.

Chapter 1

The quotation in this chapter's initial heading belongs to Joseph Margolis, *Texts Without Referents*, 38.

1. See Heidegger, "Building, Dwelling, Thinking," in *Poetry, Language, Thought*, 145–61; and Haraway, "A Cyborg Manifesto: Science, Technology, and Socialist-Feminism in the Late Twentieth Century," in *Simians, Cyborgs, and Women*, 151. See also Hayles, *How We Became Posthuman*, esp. chap. 10, "The Semiotics of Virtuality: Mapping the Posthuman," 247–82; and Janicaud, *On the Human Condition*, 34: "The Cyborg remains very human, like a big toy. You can play with it."

2. Lyotard, "After Wittgenstein," in *Political Writings*, 21.

3. Lyotard, *The Inhuman*, 2.

4. Foucault, *The Order of Things*, 387. Social constructionists hold that human subjectivity is a social formation, a historical and cultural artifact. For a closely argued account of this idea, see Margolis, *Life Without Principles*. Being human is description dependent, that is, it occurs "only under a description," and descriptions are historically and culturally contingent, that is, internal to local social practices. See Hacking, "Making Up People," esp. 230–31:

[On the] difference between people and things: what camels, mountains, and microbes are doing does not depend on our words. What happens to tuberculosis bacilli depends on whether or not we poison them with BCG vaccine, but it does not depend upon how we describe them. Of course we poison them with a certain vaccine in part because we describe them in certain ways, but it is the vaccine that kills, not our words. Human action is more closely linked to human description than bacterial action. A century ago I would have said that consumption is caused by bad air and sent the patient to the alps. Today, I may say that TB is caused by microbes and prescribe a two-year course of injections. But what is happening to the microbes and the patient is entirely independent of my correct or incorrect description, even though it is not independent of the medication prescribed. The microbes' possibilities are delimited by nature, not by words. What is curious about human action is that by and large what I am deliberately doing depends on the possibilities of description. To repeat, this is a tautological inference from what is now a philosopher's commonplace, that all intentional acts are acts under a description. Hence if new modes of description come into being, new possibilities for action come into being in consequence.

Instead of "social constructionism" Hacking speaks of "dynamic nominalism," which is just the idea that "numerous kinds of human being and human acts come into being hand in hand with our invention of categories labeling them" (236). So there will always be new possibilities as to what a human being is. See Jacques Derrida's critique of anthropocentrism, "The Ends of Man." Derrida's idea is that we can no longer isolate anything proper to human beings that sets them off from other creatures. When it comes to "man," he says, "one must speak several languages and produce several texts at once" (135).

5. See Paul Churchland, "Eliminative Materialism and the Propositional Attitude," 67–90. Cf. Stich, *From Folk Psychology to Cognitive Science*; and Patricia Churchland, *Neurophilosophy*, 299–310, esp. 302. In *Texts Without Referents*, Joseph Margolis notes that "the eliminationist does not mean to describe or explain the *human*—he eliminates it altogether; what the term 'human' appears to affirm is ultimately not (he claims) actual or real. It, too, is to be eliminated, together with the baggage of its pretended world" (xiv). In *Content and Consciousness*, Daniel Dennett says that, from the materialist's or, more accurately, the physicalist's standpoint,

> the story we tell when we tell the ordinary story of a person's mental activities cannot be mapped with precision on to the extensional story of events in the person's body, nor has the ordinary story any real precision of its own. It has no precision, for when we say a person knows or believes this or that, for example, we ascribe to him no determinable, circumscribed, invariant, generalizable states, capacities, or dispositions. The personal story, moreover, has a relatively vulnerable and impermanent place in our [physicalist] conceptual scheme, and could in principle be rendered "obsolete" if some day we ceased to *treat* anything (any mobile body or system or device) as an intentional system—by reasoning with it, communicating with it, etc. That day is not to be expected—and certainly not hoped for—in spite of the inroads that are now being made in "impersonal" ways of controlling people. (189–90)

6. Cora Diamond, "The Importance of Being Human," 36–62, esp. 52–57. Diamond's argument is that "our imaginative sense of what it is to be human" or to lead a human life is morally indispensable to human solidarity, particular with those (she emphasizes people who are retarded) who are not at all like us. See also Williams, "Making Sense of Humanity," in *Making Sense of Humanity*, 79–89; and Midgley, *Beast and Man*, esp. part 4, "Marks of Man." The term "intentional system" is Dennett's and has application to machines and life-forms of every sort; see *Brainstorms*, 3–22.

7. Cavell, *The Claim of Reason*, 416.

8. Dennett, *Consciousness Explained*, 73: "According to common agreement among philosophers, a zombie would be a human being who exhibits perfectly natural, alert, loquacious, vivacious behavior but is in fact not conscious at all, but rather some sort of automaton. The whole point of the philosopher's notion of zombie is that you can't tell a zombie from a normal person by examining external behavior. Since that is all we ever get to see of our friends and neighbors, *some of your best friends may be zombies*."

9. See Nussbaum, "The Speech of Alcibiades: A Reading of the *Symposium*," in *The Fragility of Goodness*, 198–99. The idea is that Socrates is the first embodiment of a "phil-

osophical self." "The philosophical self," according to Wittgenstein, "is not the human being, not the human body, not the human soul, with which psychology deals, but rather the metaphysical subject, the limit of the world—not a part of it" (*Tractatus* 5.641).

10. Cavell, "An Interview," 50.
11. Hegel, *Phenomenology of Spirit*, 31.
12. Kojève, *Introduction to the Reading of Hegel*, 158.
13. See Cherry, "Machines as Persons?" 24. For a more recent view of how we should respond to "biotechnology" and its products, see Sloterdijk, "Rules for the Human Zoo."
14. See Mary Midgley on "the Beast Within," *Beast and Man*, 36–44, esp. 43: "I do not think it is any accident that Plato, the first Greek who consistently wrote of the gods as good, was also the first active exponent of the Beast Within. Black horses, wolves, lions, hawks, asses, and pigs recur every time he mentions the subject of evil. This is not an idle stylistic device: there is no such thing in Plato. His serious view is that evil is something alien to the soul; something Other, the debasing effect of matter seeping in through instinctive nature."
15. Dennett, *Kinds of Minds*, 22–23. Cf. *Consciousness Explained*, 431–48.
16. Putnam, "Robots." The question of where or how robots stand within a human community is a main issue in Marge Piercy's novel *He, She, and It*, in which the progressive *homonization* of an automaton produces a dilemma for the town which it was created to defend: interaction with others, particularly the young woman assigned to instruct it in human responses, produces so human a robot that the townspeople are at a loss as to how to treat it. (Should it, for example, be allowed to vote?)
17. Cavalieri and Singer, *The Great Ape Project*.
18. Levinas, "The Rights of Man," 116.
19. See 164c: "Obviously it must be true that they are others; if it were not, we could not be talking about 'the others.' And if we are talking about the others, things that are others must be different; 'other' and 'different' are two names for the same thing. Moreover, we speak of a thing as different from, or other than, something that is different from, or other than, it. So the others must have something to be 'other than.' What can this something be? Not the one, for there is no one. They must, then, be other than each other; that is the only possibility left, if they are not to be other than nothing."
20. See Sass, "Humanism, Hermeneutics, and the Concept of the Human Subject." Theodor Adorno has an interesting thesis in his *Aesthetic Theory*, namely that "natural beauty vanished from aesthetics as a result of the burgeoning domination of the concept of freedom and human dignity, which was inaugurated by Kant and then rigorously transplanted into aesthetics by Schiller and Hegel; in accord with this concept nothing in the world is worthy of attention except that for which the autonomous subject has to thank itself" (62).
21. Levinas, *Collected Philosophical Papers*, 129.

22. Compare Margolis, "Human Space: Systems, Holisms, Structuralisms," in *Texts Without Referents*, 144–83. The "space" of modernity is, arguably, systematized, not only in the way it is construed philosophically but also in the way that it is constructed technologically, institutionally, bureaucratically, and so forth. Margolis's essay analyzes the multifarious "holisms" that our current intellectual culture uses to describe the order of things. Margolis's aim is, basically, "to get clearer about what sort of theories must be rejected in rejecting the thesis that the human world forms a system" (152). Margolis has no patience with Levinas's "ineffability" (i.e., the idea that the human cannot be conceptualized or brought under any description whatsoever), but he is closer to Levinas than he realizes. See also 37–66, on the "technological self." Margolis is a rarity—an analytic historicist (or perhaps "culturalist") who believes that human beings are socially formed, and here confronts the problem of what sort of human being is formed within a technological culture.

23. See Cadava, Connor, and Nancy, *Who Comes After the Subject?* In this volume a number of French and German thinkers, including Levinas, respond to the following question posed by Jean-Luc Nancy:

> Who comes after the subject? This question can be explained as follows: one of the major characteristics of contemporary thought is the putting into question of the instance of the "subject," according to the structure, the meaning, and the value subsumed under this term in modern thought, from Descartes to Hegel, if not to Husserl. The inaugurating decisions of contemporary thought . . . have all involved putting subjectivity on trial. A widespread discourse of recent date proclaimed the subject's simple liquidation. Everything seems, however, to point to the necessity, not of a "return to the subject" . . . but on the contrary, of a movement forward toward someone—*some one*—else in its place. . . . Who would it be? (5)

Compare the volumes of essays *Deconstructed Subjectivities*, ed. Simon Critchley and Peter Dews, and *The Modern Subject: Conceptions of the Self in Classical German Philosophy*, ed. Karl Ameriks and Dieter Sturma.

24. Sartre, *Being and Nothingness*, 340–76.

25. See Bernasconi, "'Only the Persecuted . . . ,'" 77–86. See also Bernet, "The Other in Myself."

26. See Critchley, "Prolegomena to Any Post-Deconstructive Subjectivity" (*DS*, 30): "Levinas's work offers a *material phenomenology of subjective life*, where the conscious I of representation is reduced to the sentient I of enjoyment. The self-conscious, autonomous subject of intentionality is reduced to a living subject that is subject to the conditions of its existence. Now for Levinas it is precisely this I of enjoyment that is capable of being claimed or called into question ethically by the other person. Ethics, for Levinas, is simply and entirely this calling into question of myself—of my spontaneity, of my *jouissance*, of my freedom—by the other."

27. Levinas, *Difficult Freedom*, 291–95.

28. See Hollis, *Models of Man*, 5–11, 23–39; and Cavell, *The Claim of Reason*: "We are apt to be struck with the idea of the human being as a *creature*, meaning a living thing, something procreated; but meaning equally something created. Then we seem to have the following choice. Either we attempt to give up the idea of the human being as created, in which case we attempt to *naturalize* the human being, to understand this being in relation to (nonhuman) nature, an attempt sometimes described as locating the human being's *place* in nature; or else we retain the idea of ourselves as created and attempt further to *humanize* this creation, identifying ourselves now as the creators of ourselves, since obviously no *other* being could be eligible for such a role" (465).

29. Cavell, *Conditions Handsome and Unhandsome*, xxvii. Cavell is careful to point out that this responsibility to oneself does not close out other people but requires that one make oneself intelligible to others, creating a voice of one's own that others recognize. I try to sort out the relation of self and other in Cavell's philosophy in "The Last Romantic: Stanley Cavell and the Writing of Philosophy."

30. Cavell, "Being Odd, Getting Even," in *In Quest of the Ordinary*, 108; and also *Conditions Handsome and Unhandsome*, 47–48. Cf. Marcel Mauss's distinction between the *personne* and the *moi*, in "A Category of the Human Mind: The Notion of the Person; the Notion of the Self." The *personne* (in French this also means "no one") is a social construction, an inhabitant and also an embodiment of a culture (arguably premodern: the tribesman, the peasant); the *moi* is the autonomous, self-reflexive ego capable of self-definition (arguably modern: the figure of Rousseau comes to mind).

31. Cavell seems to hold to Kant's idea that identifies humanity with autonomy. See *Conditions Handsome and Unhandsome*, where Cavell glosses Emerson's line from 'Self-Reliance" that we are only "bugs, spawn": "Our moralized shame is debarring us from the conditions of the moral life, from the possibility of responsibility over our lives, from responding to our lives rather than bearing them dumbly or justifying them automatonically. That debarment or embarrassment is for Emerson, as for Kant, a state other than the human, since it lacks the humanly defining fact of freedom. That we are perceived as 'bugs' says this and more. Bugs are not human, but they are not monsters either; bugs in human guise are inhuman, monstrous" (48). Compare Heidegger on the "they" (*das Man*) in *Being and Time*, §§25–27. See Lysaker, *Emerson and Self-Culture*.

32. See Cavell, *The Senses of Walden*, 102–10; and "Emerson's Constitutional Amending: Reading 'Fate,'" in *Philosophical Passages*, 12–41, esp. 34.

33. Recall the parable of the café waiter who turns himself into a thing: "His movement is quick and forward, a little too precise, a little too rapid. . . . Finally, there he returns, trying to imitate in his walk the inflexible stiffness of some kind of automaton while carrying his tray with the recklessness of a tightrope walker. . . . He applies himself to chaining his movements as if they were mechanisms, the one regulating the other; his gestures and even his voice seem to be mechanisms; he gives himself the

quickness and pitiless rapidity of things.... Society demands that he limit himself to his function" (*BN*, 101–2).

34. See Bowen and Stone, "'Making the Human' in Sartre's Unpublished Dialectical Ethics."

35. Sartre, "Existentialism Is a Humanism."

36. Foucault, *History of Sexuality*, vol. 3, esp. 37–68.

37. Foucault, "What Is Enlightenment?" in *Essential Works*, vol. 1, 312.

38. Rorty, "The Contingency of Selfhood," in *Contingency, Irony, and Solidarity*, 27–28. On romantic irony as "living poetically," see Kierkegaard, *The Concept of Irony*, 279–332. See especially Friedrich Schlegel, *Philosophical Fragments*: "A really free and cultivated person ought to be able to attune himself at will to being philosophical or philological, critical or poetical, historical or rhetorical, ancient or modern: quite arbitrarily, just as one tunes an instrument at any time and to any degree" (Fr. 55).

39. See Preston, "The Public and the Private Appeal of Self-Fashioning," 10–19.

40. Frank, "Is Subjectivity a Non-Thing?" in Ameriks and Sturma, *The Modern Subject*, 187–88.

41. Levinas, *Of God Who Comes to Mind*, 173–74.

42. A statement that Paul Ricoeur, among others, finds intolerable. See Ricoeur, *Oneself as Another*, 335–41. In *Otherwise Than Being*, Ricoeur complains, Levinas employs "hyperbole to the point of paroxysm" (338). Ricoeur's interest is in narrative as a mode of self-construction: I am not I until I can give an account of myself. See the chapter "The Self and Narrative Identity" (140–68).

43. Agamben, *Homo Sacer*, 1–12. See Michael Marder, "Taming the Beast: The Other Tradition in Political Theory." Marder sensibly asks why animals (rather than outcast humans) are not a prime example of "bare life" (48).

44. See Tournier, *Vendredi*, 36 / *Friday*, 38:

He discovered that for all of us the presence of other people [*autrui*] is a powerful element of distraction, not only because they constantly break up our activities and interrupt our train of thought, but because the mere possibility of their doing so illumines a world of concerns situated at the edge of our consciousness but capable at any moment of becoming its center. That marginal and almost ghostly [*fantomatique*] presence of things with which he was not immediately concerned had gradually vanished from Robinson's mind. He was now surrounded by objects subject only to the arbitrary law of all or nothing, and thus it was that, being wholly absorbed in the business of building the ship, he had completely overlooked the problem of launching her.

See Deleuze, "Michel Tournier and the World Without Others," 306: "What happens when Others [*autrui*] are missing from the structure of the world? In that case, there reigns alone the brutal opposition of the sun and the earth, of an unbearable light and an obscure abyss: the 'summary law of all or nothing.' The known and the unknown, the perceived and the unperceived confront one another in a battle without nuances.... A harsh and black world, without potentialities or virtualities: the category of the possible has collapsed."

45. Bataille, *The Accursed Share*, vols. 2 and 3, 198.

46. See Derrida's essay on Bataille, "From Restricted to General Economy: A Hegelianism Without Reserve," in *Writing and Difference*: "For sovereignty has no identity, is not *self, for itself, toward itself, near itself.* In order not to govern, that is to say, in order not to be subjugated, it *must* subordinate nothing (direct object), that is to say, be subordinated to *nothing or no one* . . . ; it must expend itself without reserve, lose itself, lose consciousness, lose all memory of itself and all the interiority of itself . . . ; and, as the ultimate subversion of lordship, it must no longer seek to be recognized" (265).

Chapter 2

The quotation in this chapter's first heading is from "What Are Masterpieces and Why Are There So Few of Them?" in Gertrude Stein, *Writings and Lectures*, 149.

1. Ovid, *Metamorphoses*, 79.

2. In Maurice Blanchot's work this is the temporality of the "between," or *entretemps*, as in the figure of *le pas au delà*—"Let there be a past, let there be a future, with nothing that would allow the passage from one to the other." See Blanchot, *The Step Not Beyond*, 12.

3. Charlotte F. Otten, ed., *A Lycanthropy Reader: Werewolves in Western Culture*, esp. Rosenstock and Vincent, "A Case of Lycanthropy," 31–34. There is a harrowing case history, "The Wolf! The Wolf!" in *The Seminar of Jacques Lacan, I: Freud's Papers on Technique 1953–54*, in which a young child experiences himself as a wolf. Cf. Freud, *Totem and Taboo*, chap. 4, "The Return of Totemism in Childhood," esp. 126–27: "There is a great deal of resemblance between the relations of children and of primitive men toward animals. Children show no trace of the arrogance which urges adult civilized men to draw a hard and fast line between their own nature and that of all other animals. Children have no scruples over allowing animals to rank as their full equals. Uninhibited as they are in the avowal of their bodily needs, they no doubt feel themselves more akin to animals than to their elders, who may well be a puzzle to them." See also Baring-Gould, *The Book of Were-Wolves*, and Douglas, *The Beast Within*.

4. "Monster Culture (Seven Theses)," in Cohen, *Monster Theory*, 3–25. Compare Noël Carroll's *The Philosophy of Horror; or, Paradoxes of the Heart*. Indispensable is Stephen T. Asma's *On Monsters: An Unnatural History of Our Worst Fears*.

5. Elaine Scarry has a nice paragraph on the kind of metamorphosis one is apt to see in the Scriptures. After citing a number of passages on the hardening of the heart or the stiffening of the neck, she writes: "In all of the passages cited above, the withholding of the body—the stiffening of the neck, the turning of the shoulder, the closing of the ears, the hardening of the heart, the making of the face like stone—necessitates God's forceful shattering of the reluctant human surface and repossession of the

interior." See Scarry, *The Body in Pain*, 203–4. In the Bible the human is vulnerable not to transformation into something alien but to the physical alteration of the body through wounds inflicted by (ultimately) God.

6. Greek tragedy might be thought of as the trespass of a male hero who embodies the definition of the human into an alien feminine space that marks the borderline of the human or where the definition cannot be sustained. Froma Zeitlin is thinking somewhat along these lines in her essay "Playing the Other: Theater, Theatricality, and the Feminine in Greek Drama."

7. Frye, *Anatomy of Criticism*, 33–34.

8. Musil, *The Man Without Qualities*, 34.

9. Kontos, "The World Disenchanted," 227. See Georg Simmel's famous essay "The Metropolis and Mental Life"; Simmel's thesis is that the city evacuates human subjectivity but paradoxically provokes eccentric behavior as a mode of individual self-preservation.

10. Deleuze and Guattari, *Kafka*, 14.

11. Kafka in his diaries speaks of the "complete citizen" who cannot be separated from his property ("whoever destroys the connexion destroys him at the same time"). Kafka, *Diaries*, 23.

12. The French writer Maurice Blanchot gives us a slightly more up-to-date version of Kafkaesque metamorphosis in *Thomas the Obscure*, in which the eponymous character happens at one point to be reading a book whose words suddenly begin reading *him*, setting in motion a process of consumption that turns him into an obscure lexicon:

> For hours he remained motionless, with, from time to time, the word "eyes" in place of his eyes: he was inert, captivated and unveiled. And even later when, having abandoned himself and, contemplating his book he recognized himself with disgust in the form of the text he was reading, he retained the thought that (while, perched upon his shoulders, the word *He* and the word *I* were beginning their carnage) there remained within his person which was already deprived of its senses obscure words, disembodied souls and angels of words, which were exploring him deeply. (26)

13. Lacan, *Écrits*, 131–35.

14. See Serres, *The Parasite*, which pictures the human organism as, essentially, an ecological system of parasitic inhabitants:

> It happens, in particular, that an infectious disease is provoked by the arrival of a parasite, a virus, a protozoan, a metazoan, or a fungus. Introduced either permanently or temporarily in the organism of its host that is henceforth its environment, it intercepts flows, sometimes accelerating them, turning them in its favor at every level. This one is specific—in the digestive tract—for the oral cavity or for intestinal movement; that one is specific for the circulation of blood; a third is specific for the sebaceous glands; I shall stop this enumeration, which would last for volumes on end. The sum or synopsis of

these living creatures and their activities would tell us, I guess, that there are no channels, paths, or flows, that, at least in principle, do not have their intercepters. Each one has its niche, and few niches remain unoccupied. (198)

15. Dennett's "anthropology," just to call it that, pictures us as intentional systems to be described in physiological rather than phenomenological language. The problem is that physicalists sometimes cheat when describing how the brain works by appropriating phenomenological language, and so often figure the brain as inhabited by a little man—a homunculus—who experiences brain processes as mental events. See Dennett, *Consciousness Explained*, esp. 261–62. ("Homunculi—demons, agents—are the coin of the realm in Artificial Intelligence, and computer science more generally.")

16. In *The Third Chimpanzee: The Evolution and the Future of the Human Animal*, Jared Diamond, summarizing a good deal of research, notes that chimps are genetically closer to humans than to gorillas and apes: "For example, the common and pygmy chimps differ in about 0.7 percent of their DNA and diverged around three million years ago; we differ in 1.6 percent of our DNA from either chimp and diverged from their common ancestor around seven million years ago; and gorillas differ in about 2.3 percent of their DNA from us and from chimps and diverged from the common ancestor leading to us and the two chimps around ten million years ago" (21). We are, genetically, a third species of chimpanzee. See Tyler, "Four Hands Good, Two Hands Bad," for a good reading of "Report to the Academy" and on the physiological proximity of humans and chimpanzees, who (in contrast, like us, to other primates) do not have prehensile feet. (The issue of *Parallax* in which this article appears, by the way, is a special number devoted to "the question of the animal.") See also Dawkins, "Gaps in the Mind," 80–87.

17. Melehy, "Silencing the Animals," 275.

18. See, for example, Wolfe, *Zoontologies*; Atterton and Calarco, *Animal Philosophy*; Marder, "Taming the Beast"; and Aaltola, "Personhood and Animals."

19. On the complexity of horror, see Georges Bataille, the philosopher of "extreme experiences" for whom "the fullness of horror and joy coincide." *My Mother, Madame Edwarda, The Dead Man*, 141. This paradox or antinomy is discussed below in Chapter 3.

20. Villiers de l'Isle-Adam, *Tomorrow's Eve*, 82. The French text is not always easy to find but is available online at Project Gutenberg, http://www.gutenberg.org/etext/26681.

21. Compare Marge Piercy's novel *He, She, and It*, in which a young woman named Shira is given the task of interacting with a cyborg named Yod in order to humanize it, that is, teach it how to respond to things and to others like a human being (in other words, how to have feelings). Naturally, Yod excels mere humans in everything human, including, as Shira discovers, lovemaking.

22. Agamben, *The Open*, 26–27.

Chapter 3

1. On Foucault's later work, see in particular Connolly, "Beyond Good and Evil"; and Huffer, "Foucault's Ethical *Ars Poetica*."
2. "Maurice Florence," "Michel Foucault, 1926–," trans. Catherine Porter, in Gutting, *Cambridge Companion to Foucault*, 317. In his preface to this volume Gary Gutting writes: "The article is signed with the name 'Maurice Florence,' a personnage of whom I can find no other trace on the French philosophical scene. There is, in fact, good reason to think that 'Maurice Florence' is a pseudonym and that Michel Foucault was himself the author . . . of the piece" (viii).
3. Deleuze, *Différence et repetition*, 79 / *Difference and Repetition*, 56.
4. See Blanchot, "The Relation of the Third Kind (Man Without Horizon)" (*EI*, 94–105/*IC*, 66–74). This essay is part of Blanchot's ongoing dialogue, and perhaps disagreement, with Emmanuel Levinas concerning the question of alterity, "Who Is '*Autrui*'?" For Levinas, the Other can only be another man, but for Blanchot the Other is outside all horizons, whence "it follows . . . that the Other man who is '*autrui*' also risks being always Other than man, close to what cannot be close to me: close to death, close to the night, and certainly as repulsive as anything that comes to me from these regions without horizon" (*EI*, 103/*IC*, 72). See Bruns, *Maurice Blanchot*, esp. 116–17.
5. See "On the Genealogy of Ethics" (*DEII*, 1437/*E*, 263), as well as the interview with Stephen Riggins in which Foucault remarks that he is "not a really good academic": "For me, intellectual work is related to what you could call 'aestheticism,' meaning transforming yourself [*la transformation de soi*]" (*DEII*, 1354/*E*, 130). See also Foucault, *The Hermeneutics of the Subject*.
6. See Jean-Luc Nancy, *Being Singular Plural*: "The concept of the singular implies singularization and, therefore, its distinction from other singularities (which is different from any concept of the individual, since an immanent totality, without an other, would be a perfect individual, and is also different from any concept of the particular, since this assumes the togetherness of which the particular is a part, so that such a particular can only present its difference from other particulars as numerical difference)" (*ESP*, 50/*BSP*, 32).
7. Hegel, *Phenomenology of Spirit*, 51.
8. See Bruns, "Foucault's Modernism: Language, Poetry, and the Experience of Freedom," 57–78. An earlier version of this essay appeared in Gutting, *Cambridge Companion to Foucault*, 2nd ed., 348–78.
9. Foucault, "For an Ethics of Discomfort," 137.
10. Adorno, *Aesthetic Theory*, 114.
11. See Deleuze, *Foucault*, 105–6.
12. "Michel Foucault as I Imagine Him," in Foucault and Blanchot, *Foucault/Blanchot*, 84.
13. Agamben, *The Man Without Content*, 55.

14. Sloterdijk, "Rules for the Human Zoo," 12–28, esp. 18.

15. See Tyler, "Deviants, Donestre, and Debauchees." In the background of Foucault's interest in the abnormals is the early work of Georges Bataille on "base materialism," heterology, and monsters—among other examples of the formless and repulsive against which human beings try to define themselves. See, for example, "The Deviations of Nature," in *Visions of Excess*, 53–56.

16. Foucault, *Abnormal*, 25–26, 161–63.

17. See also Gutting, "Foucault's Philosophy of Experience"; and O'Leary, "Foucault, Experience, Literature."

18. Foucault, *I, Pierre Rivière*, 195. The citation is from Peter and Favret, "The Animal, the Madman, and Death," one of the "notes" appended to Rivière's memoir and a "dossier" of legal and medical texts devoted to Rivière's case.

19. Foucault, *Herculine Barbin*, xiii.

20. See in particular Blanchot's *Le dernier homme* (*The Last Man*). The last man is a figure of non-identity, without attributes or definition—someone all the more uncanny because of his effect on those around him. As the narrator says, "he made each of us into someone else" (*DH*, 26/*LM*, 12). See Bruns, *Maurice Blanchot*, 131–35.

21. The experience of the *outside* as "desubjectivation" is something like a first-person experience of one's loss of the ability to say "I"; that is, one is no longer in a position to say, "I think." This is not so much a death-of-the-author event as it is a critique of the subject. For example, in "La pensée du dehors" Foucault quite rightly observes that, for Blanchot, "I speak" (it would be more accurate to say "I write") is not symmetrical with "I think": "'I think' led to the indubitable certainty of the 'I' and its existence; 'I speak,' on the other hand, distances, disperses, effaces that existence and lets only its empty emplacement appear. Thought about thought, an entire tradition wider than philosophy, has taught us that thought leads to the deepest interiority. Speech about speech [i.e., the so-called self-reflexivity of modern literature] leads us . . . to the outside in which the speaking subject disappears" (*DEI*, 549/*A*, 149).

22. Hadot, *Philosophy as a Way of Life*, 211: "What I am afraid of is that, by focusing his interpretation too exclusively on the culture of the self, the care of the self, and conversion toward the self—M. Foucault is propounding a culture of the self which is *too* aesthetic. In other words, this may be a new form of Dandyism, late twentieth-century style." See also Ure, "Senecan Moods: Foucault and Nietzsche on the Art of the Self." More sympathetic to Foucault's "aesthetics of the self" is Seppä, "Foucault, Enlightenment, and the Aesthetics of the Self."

23. The Apache in Baudelaire is the urban ruffian who keeps out of sight rather than the Dandy who puts himself on display. See Benjamin, *Charles Baudelaire*, 78–79: The Apache "represents the characteristics which Bounoure sees in Baudelaire's solitude—'a *noli me tangere*, an encapsulation of the individual in his difference.' The apache abjures virtue and laws; he terminates the *contrat social* forever."

24. Lacan, "The *Jouissance* of Transgression," 201. See also Braunstein, "Desire and Jouissance in the Teachings of Lacan," esp. 106–7: "Jouissance . . . does not point to anything, nor does it serve any purpose whatsoever; it is an unpredictable experience, beyond the pleasure principle." See Kristeva, "Bataille, Experience, and Practice."

25. Bataille, "Hegel, Death, and Sacrifice," 25. In *The Ethics of Psychoanalysis* Lacan says that *"jouissance* implies precisely the acceptance of death" (189). See Baudrillard, "Death in Bataille."

26. Compare Blanchot's "The Instant of My Death," in which he recalls the moment, during the last days of the Occupation, when he faced a German firing squad: "I know—do I know—that the one at whom the Germans were already aiming, awaiting but the final order, experienced then a feeling of extraordinary lightness, a sort of beatitude (nothing happy, however)—sovereign elation [*allégresse souveraine*]? The encounter of death with death?" (Blanchot/Derrida, *The Instant of My Death / Demeure*, 5).

27. Bataille, "Celestial Bodies," 78.

28. Bataille, *My Mother, Madame Edwarda, The Dead Man*, 141.

29. See Kojève, *Introduction to the Reading of Hegel*, 222: "[Man] lives *humanly* . . . only to the extent that he *negates* this natural or animal given."

30. See Bataille's "History of Eroticism" in *The Accursed Share*, esp. part 4, "Transgression" (*AS*, 89–122).

Chapter 4

This chapter first appeared in *New Literary History*, 8, no. 4 (Autumn 2007): 708–20. © *New Literary History*, The University of Virginia. Reprinted by permission.

1. On Deleuze and Guattari's conception of the state, see Patton, "Conceptual Politics and the War-Machine in *Mille Plateaux*"; and May, *The Political Philosophy of Poststructuralist Anarchism*, 104–8.

2. Deleuze, *The Logic of Sense*, 1.

3. Bataille, "The Psychological Structure of Fascism" (*VE*, 142). Specifically, the *"heterogeneous* world includes everything resulting from *unproductive* expenditure" (*dépense*, or expenditure without return), that is, whatever lies outside the systems of exchange that constitute the bourgeois order of things. See Bataille, "The Notion of Expenditure [*Dépense*]" (*VE*, 116–29).

4. See Krell, "All You Can't Eat," which is Krell's notes on a course taught by Jacques Derrida on various (unmentionable) themes of eating and excretion.

5. Kristeva, *Powers of Horror*, 3.

6. See also Bataille, "Hegel, Death, and Sacrifice." The "certain reading of Hegel" refers to Alexandre Kojève's famous lectures on *The Phenomenology of the Spirit* in Paris during the 1930s, *Introduction to the Reading of Hegel*, esp. 222: "Negativity is nothing other than human *Freedom*—that is, that by which Man differs from animal. . . . [Man]

can exist freely as an animal in a given natural World. But he lives *humanly* in it only to the extent that he negates this natural or animal given."

7. See Franck, *Chair et corps*; and Nancy, *Corpus*. See Caputo's pages on flesh in *Against Ethics: Contributions to a Poetics of Obligation with Constant Reference to Deconstruction*, esp. 194–219.

8. Paul Valéry once distinguished among *three* bodies: The first is *my* body, that is, the one that I inhabit, experience, suffer, clothe, and clean; the second is "the one others see, and that is more or less revealed in the glass or in portraits"; the third is perhaps most flesh-like "since we only know it from having divided it and taken it to pieces. It must be drawn and quartered before it can be known. Out of it flow scarlet or pale or hyaline liquids, often extremely viscous. Out of it are removed masses of various dimensions which have been fitted in rather neatly: these are sponges, vessels, tubes, filaments, articulated bars.... All this, reduced to very thin slices or to drops, reveals under the microscope the shapes of corpuscles which look like nothing at all.... And what relation there can possibly be between these tiny constellations with delicate radicles, and sensation and thought?" Valéry, *Selected Writings*, 232–33. Jean-Luc Nancy captures something of the idea of flesh when he writes: "*Body* would then first be the experience of *its own weight* (of its matter, its mass, its pulp, its grain, its gaping, its mole, its molecule, its turf, its turgidity, its fiber, its juice, its invagination, its volume, its fall, its meat, its coagulation, its dough, its crystallinity, its twitching, its spasm, its unknotting, its tissue, its dwelling, its disorder, its promiscuity, its smell, its taste, its resonance, its resolution, its reason)." See "Corpus" (*BP*, 200).

9. Maurice Merleau-Ponty gives us something like a Greek theory of flesh in *The Visible and the Invisible*, where flesh is the circle of touching and being touched that connects me to the world, which is made of flesh as much as I am. The project here is to get around behind the back of the mind-body problem. Merleau-Ponty writes:

[The] flesh we are speaking of is not matter. It is the coiling over of the visible upon the seeing body, of the tangible upon the touching body, which is attested in particular when the body sees itself, touches itself seeing and touching the things, such that, simultaneously, *as* tangible it descends among them, *as* touching it dominates them all and draws its relationship and even this double relationship from itself, by dehiscence or fission of its own mass. This concentration of the visibles about one of them, or this bursting forth of the mass of the body toward the things, which makes a vibration of my skin become the sleek and the rough, makes me *follow with my eyes* the movements and the contours of the things themselves, this magical relation, this pact between them and me according to which I lend them my body in order that they inscribe upon it and give me their resemblance, this fold, this central cavity of the visible which is my vision, these two mirror arrangements of the seeing and the visible, the touching and the touched, form a close-bound system that I count on, define a vision in general and a constant style of visibility from which I cannot detach myself, even when a particular vision turns out to be illusory, for I remain certain in that case that in looking closer I would have had the true vision, and that in any case, whether it be this one or another, *there is a true vision*. (146–47) This is at least a very upright conception of the flesh—notice that I "dominate things" by touching them; and of course touching and being touched are finally ocularcentric, that is, the tangible resolves into the visible, as if the flesh were reducible to the relation of hand and eye. Compare Derrida's "Exemplary Stories of the 'Flesh'" in *On Touching—Jean-Luc Nancy*, 135–262, esp. (1) 182–215, which is a commentary on Merleau-Ponty's *The Visible and the Invisible*; (2) pp. 216–43, on Didier Franck's *Chair et corps*; and (3) 244–62, on Jean-Louis Chrétien's *L'appel et la réponse*. Interestingly, the flesh in French thought seems to be informed by a constant allusion to the doctrine of Incarnation (hence more Christian than Jewish)—see *On Touching*, 219–24.

10. See in particular Bataille's essay "The Notion of Expenditure," in which gambling, the wearing of sumptuous jewelry, kinky sex, but also theater and poetry are given as examples of *dépense*: "The term poetry, applied to the least degraded and least intellectualized forms of expression of the state of loss, can be considered synonymous with expenditure [*dépense*]; it in fact signifies, in the most precise way, creation by means of loss. Its meaning is therefore close to that of *sacrifice*" (*VE*, 125). This is because in poetry words are not exchanged for meanings; poetry is rather the experience of the sheer *materiality* of language. See McCaffery, "Writing as a General Economy," in *North of Intention*, 201–21.

11. See also Deleuze, "Desire and Pleasure," 183–94.

12. No doubt they realized that it would be hard to follow Derrida's essay on Artaud's theory, "The Theater of Cruelty and the Closure of Representation," in *Writing and Difference*, 232–50. See, however, Deleuze's essay on Carlo Bene's "theater of subtraction," "One Manifesto Less."

13. Adams, "Operation Orlan," in *The Emptiness of the Image*, 145. Compare Michel Serres on the "phantomatic face": "The make-up girl covers the face to be seen on television with a viscous cream, and it is not, as we think, a simple matter of lighting, it is that the public man dons the theatrical mask, which the Latins called persona. You who enter here, erase all difference, leave aside any singularity. Might as well be done with them once for all, and give your skin that pure capacity for multiplicity. Might as well not be anybody anymore, a pure abstract phantom that every viewer thinks he recognizes. This one who lets himself be seen by the multitude is also in search of ichnography." See Serres, *Genesis*, 28–29. See also Wegenstein, "Getting Under the Skin, or, How Faces Have Become Obsolete."

14. See Rose, "Is It Art?"; Moos, "Memories of Being"; Ince, *Orlan: Millennial Female*; Cros et al., *Orlan: Carnal Art*; and O'Bryan, *Carnal Art*.

15. Compare Giorgio Agamben, for whom the difference between fable and mystery is a difference between the open mouth and the closed: "The silence of the mystery is undergone as a rupture, plunging man back into the pure, mute language of

nature; but as a spell, silence must eventually be shattered and conquered. This is why, in the fairy tale, man is struck dumb, and animals emerge from the pure language of nature in order to speak. Through the temporary confusion of the two spheres, it is the world of the *open mouth*, of the Indo-European root **bha* (from which the word fable is derived), which the fairy tale validates, against the world of the *closed mouth*, of the root **mu*" (*IH*, 70).

16. See Sylvester, *The Brutality of Fact*, 23, 46.

17. In Deleuze and Guattari's theory, the declension of the face never crosses the boundary into the absolutely nonhuman. The faces of all creatures are subject to the abstract machine of faciality just as ours are. Philosophers sometimes call this "speciesism," in which mental predicates are ascribed to nonhuman animals. In *Real People*, Kathleen Wilkes gives a nice example:

> Appearance is important: the pig, a highly intelligent animal, is allowed fewer [mental predicates] than is the comparatively stupid koala—the koala's face is a little bit like ours, whereas the pig does not look much like us, and its squeal is less like the human's cry of pain than is, say, the yelp of a dog (which is again less intelligent than the pig). So looking or sounding like us helps; and there is a second reason, too: familiarity. Those animals that spend much of their time with us, like cats and dogs, receive a greater allocation of mental predicates than do those that are comparatively strange. (97)

18. See Jardine, "Women in Limbo"; Grosz, "A Thousand Tiny Sexes"; Goulmari, "A Minortarian Feminism?"; and Braidotti, "Becoming Woman."

19. Schmiedel, "With or Without Lacan?" 19.

20. For Deleuze and Guattari, of course, we are only machines—desiring machines, production machines. *Anti-Oedipus* begins with a description of Georg Büchner's schizoid, Lenz, in a moment of freedom in the forest: "Lenz has projected himself back to a time before the man-nature dichotomy, before all the co-ordinates based on this fundamental dichotomy have been laid down. He does not live nature as nature, but as a process of production. There is no such thing as either man or nature now, only a process that produces the one within the other and couples the machines together. Producing machines, desiring machines everywhere, schizophrenic machines, all of species life: the self and the non-self, outside and inside, no longer have any meaning whatsoever" (*AO*, 2). Reference is to Büchner's short story *Lenz* (1836).

21. See Hacking, "Making Up People."

22. Aaltola, "Personhood and Animals," 180. See Cavalieri and Singer, *The Great Ape Project* (London: Fourth Estate, 1994), esp. 230–79.

23. The two stories that make up *The Lives of Animals* were presented as the Tanner Lectures at Princeton's University Center for Human Values. The volume contains an introduction by Amy Gutman and responses by scholars from various disciplines: Marjorie Garber, Peter Singer, Wendy Doniger, and (in particular) Barbara Smuts, who is cited below.

Chapter 5

1. Derrida, *L'animal que donc je suis*. Papers for the entire conference were published under the title *L'animal autobiographique*. Derrida's lectures (nearly ten hours' worth) consist of, among other things, close readings of philosophical texts on "the animal" from Aristotle, Descartes, and Kant to Heidegger, Levinas, and Lacan. An English translation of the first lecture, "The Animal That Therefore I Am (More to Follow)," by David Wills, appeared in *Critical Inquiry*, 28, no. 4 (Winter 2002), 369–418. A translation by David Wills of the third lecture, "And Say the Animal Responded?" appeared in *Zoontologies: The Question of the Animal*, ed. Cary Wolfe (Minneapolis: University of Minnesota Press, 2004), 121–46. Both texts, with revised translations by David Wills, were published in *The Animal That I Therefore Am*, ed. Marie-Louise Mallet (New York: Fordham University Press, 2008). See Wolfe's discussion of Derrida on the animal in his contribution to that volume, "In the Shadow of Wittgenstein's Lion: Language, Ethics, and the Question of the Animal," 1–57, esp. 19–34. Wolfe's essay first appeared in his *Animal Rites: American Culture, the Discourse of Species, and Posthumanist Theory*, 44–97.

2. See Rapaport, *The Later Derrida*, 100.

3. See Derrida, "'Eating Well,' or the Calculation of the Subject," esp. 110–11, on the openness or indefiniteness of the *who*. Derrida cites a passage from Blanchot's *L'amitié* (on the peculiar "personless presence" of Bataille's use of the personal pronoun "I"): "And when we ask ourselves the question, 'Who was the subject of this experience?' this question is perhaps already an answer if, even to him who led it, the experience asserted itself in this interrogative form, by substituting the openness of a 'Who?' without answer for the closed and singular 'I'; not that this means that he had simply to ask himself 'What is this I that I am?' but much more radically to recover himself without reprieve, no longer as 'I' but as a 'Who?,' the unknown and slippery being of an indefinite 'Who?'" This is taken from the essay "Friendship," in *Friendship*, 291.

4. Rilke, *The Selected Poems*, 64–65.

5. See Lacan, "The Mirror Phase as Formative of the Function of the I," in *Écrits*, 1–8. In contrast to the human infant, the chimpanzee, according to Lacan, takes no interest in its image, which is to say no self-image ever forms. In other words, an animal cannot become a subject—cannot traverse the boundary between the imaginary and symbolic orders, and therefore cannot dissemble, which would mean taking an other into account. The animal cannot respond to (or as) an other. In "And Say the Animal Responded?" Derrida does not so much dispute this thesis as examine the "fragility" of the oppositions on which it depends, "beginning with that between the symbolic and imaginary which underwrites, finally, this whole anthropocentric reinstitution of the superiority of the human order over the animal order" (*LAN*, 186/*ANT*, 138).

6. Heidegger, *What Is Called Thinking?* 61. Also: "The hand is a peculiar thing. In the common view, the hand is part of our bodily organism. But the hand's essence can never be determined, or explained, by its being an organ which can grasp. Apes,

too, have organs that can grasp, but they do not have hands. The hand is infinitely different from all grasping organs—paws, claws, or fangs—different by an abyss of essence. Only a being who can speak, that is, think, can have hands and can be handy in achieving works of handicraft" (16). See Derrida, "*Geschlect* II." See also Elden, "Heidegger's Animals," esp. 278: "The animal is different from the human, who is the *zoon lógon échon* [sic]. It is for [this reason] that animals do not dwell or abide; neither do they look [*blacken*], but rather they peer, glare, gawk or gape, because there is not a 'self-disclosure of being,' nothing is disclosed to it . . . ; equally the pet dog does not really 'eat,' and does not really comport itself to the table it lies under or the stairs it runs up."

7. Calarco, "Deconstruction Is Not Vegetarianism," 182.

8. See Blanchot, "The Limit-Experience":

[It] must be understood that possibility is not the sole dimension of our experience, and it is perhaps given to us to "live" each of the events that is ours by way of a double relation. We live it one time as something we comprehend, grasp, bear, and master . . . ; we live it another time as something that escapes all employ and all end, and more, as that which escapes our very capacity to undergo it, but whose trial we cannot escape. (*EI*, 307–8/*IC*, 207)

9. See Bataille, *L'expérience intérieure*, 68 / *Inner Experience*, 54; and Blanchot, *L'écriture du desastre*, 176–79 / *The Writing of the Disaster*, 114–16).

10. See Derrida's discussion of the conundrum of the child who "speaks before knowing how to speak" in *Of Grammatology*, 247–48.

11. See Foucault, *The Order of Things*, 65: In literature "language . . . exists in its raw and primitive being [*être brut et primitive*], in the simple, material form of writing, a stigma upon things, a mark imprinted across the world which is part of its most ineffaceable forms." Foucault's idea is that in the nineteenth century (i.e., with the beginning of modernism) literature "ceased to belong to the order of discourse and became the manifestation of language in its thickness" (265). See also "A Preface to Transgression," on "the extreme forms of language in which Bataille, Maurice Blanchot, and Pierre Klossowski have made their home" (*DEI*, 168/*A*, 76); and Lecercle, *Philosophy Through the Looking-Glass*, 80.

12. In *A Taste for the Secret* Derrida writes: "My own experience of writing leads me to think that one does not always write with a desire to be understood—that there is a paradoxical desire not to be understood. It's not simple, but there is a certain 'I hope that not everyone understands everything about this text,' because if such a transparency of intelligibility were ensured it would destroy the text" (*TS*, 30).

13. Here it would be useful to consult the texts gathered together in Cavalieri and Singer, *The Great Apes Project*, especially Francine Patterson and Wendy Gordon, "The Case for the Personhood of Gorillas" (58–77), with its description of Koko, who uses sign language to initiate conversations with humans, who recognizes herself in the mirror and enjoys making faces at herself, who can lie, and who understands what it is to die.

14. See, for example, Derrida, "A Silkworm of One's Own."
15. Compare Acampora and Acampora, *A Nietzsche Bestiary*.
16. Derrida, "The Ends of Man," 135.
17. See Sunstein and Nussbaum, "Beyond 'Compassion and Humanity': Justice for Nonhuman Animals," in *Animal Rights*, 306. An expanded version of this essay appears in Nussbaum, *Frontiers of Justice: Disability, Nationality, Species Membership* (Cambridge, MA: Harvard University Press, 2006), 325–405.
18. Cora Diamond, *The Realistic Spirit*, 328–30.
19. Levinas, *Difficult Freedom*, 152.
20. Derrida, "Hostipitality," 7–8.
21. Derrida, *Monolinguism of the Other*, 66.

Works Cited

Aaltola, Elisa. "Personhood and Animals: Three Approaches." *Environmental Ethics*, 30, no. 2 (2008): 175–93.
Acampora, Christa Davis, and Ralph R. Acampora. *A Nietzsche Bestiary: Becoming Animal Beyond Docile and Brutal*. Lanham, MD: Rowman & Littlefield, 2004.
Adams, Parveen. *The Emptiness of the Image*. London: Routledge, 1991.
Adorno, Theodor. *Aesthetic Theory*. Trans. Robert Hullot-Kentor. Minneapolis: University of Minnesota Press, 1997.
———. "Vers une musique informelle." In *Quasi Una Fantasia: Essays on Modern Music*, trans. Rodney Livingstone, pp. 269–322. London: Verso, 1998.
Agamben, Giorgio. *Homo Sacer: Sovereign Power and Bare Life*. Trans. Daniel Heller-Roazen. Stanford, CA: Stanford University Press, 1998.
———. *Infancy and History: On the Destruction of Experience*. Trans. Liz Heron. London: Verso, 1993.
———. *The Man Without Content*. Trans. Georgia Albert. Stanford, CA: Stanford University Press, 1999.
———. *The Open: Man and Animal*. Trans. Kevin Attell. Stanford, CA: Stanford University Press, 2004.
Ameriks, Karl, and Dieter Sturma, eds. *The Modern Subject: Conceptions of the Self in Classical German Philosophy*. Albany: SUNY Press, 1995.
Artaud, Antonin. *Antonin Artaud: Selected Writings*. Trans. Helen Weaver. Ed. Susan Sontag. Berkeley: University of California Press, 1988.
Asma, Stephen T. *On Monsters: An Unnatural History of Our Worst Fears*. Oxford: Oxford University Press, 2009.
Atterton, Peter, and Matthew Calarco, eds. *Animal Philosophy: Ethics and Identity*. New York: Continuum, 2004.
Baring-Gould, Sabine. *The Book of Were-Wolves: Being an Account of a Terrible Superstition*. London: Smith-Elder, 1865.
Bataille, Georges. *The Accursed Share: An Essay on General Economy*, vols. 2 and 3. Trans. Robert Hurley. New York: Zone Books, 1993.
———. *The Bataille Reader*. Ed. Fred Botting and Scott Wilson. Oxford: Basil Blackwell, 1997.

———. "Celestial Bodies." Trans. Annette Michelson. *October*, 36 (Spring 1986): 75–78.
———. *L'expérience intérieure*. Paris: Gallimard, 1954.
———. "Hegel, Death, and Sacrifice." Trans. Jonathan Strauss. In *On Bataille*, ed. Allan Stoekl. Yale French Studies, no. 78 (1990): 9–28.
———. *Inner Experience*. Trans. Leslie Anne Boldt. Albany: SUNY Press, 1998.
———. *My Mother, Madame Edwarda, The Dead Man*. Trans. Austryn Wainhouse. London: Marion Boyars, 1995.
———. *Visions of Excess: Selected Writings, 1927–1939*. Trans. Allan Stoekl. Minneapolis: University of Minnesota Press, 1985.
Baudrillard, Jean. "Death in Bataille." In *Bataille: A Critical Reader*, ed. Fred Botting and Scott Wilson, pp. 139–45. Oxford: Blackwell, 1998.
Benjamin, Walter. *Charles Baudelaire: A Lyric Poet in the Era of High Capitalism*. Trans. Harry Zohn. London: Verso, 1983.
Bernasconi, Robert. "'Only the Persecuted . . . ': Language of the Oppressor, Language of the Oppressed." In *Ethics as First Philosophy: The Significance of Emmanuel Levinas for Philosophy, Literature, and Religion*, ed. Adriaan Peperzak, pp. 77–86. New York: Routledge, 1995.
Bernet, Rudolf. "The Other in Myself." In *Deconstructed Subjectivities*, ed. Simon Critchley and Peter Dews, pp. 169–84. Albany: SUNY Press, 1996.
Blanchot, Maurice. *L'amitié*. Paris: Gallimard, 1971.
———. *Le dernier homme*. Paris: Gallimard, 1953.
———. *L'écriture du désastre*. Paris: Gallimard, 1980.
———. *L'entretien infini*. Paris: Gallimard, 1969.
———. *L'espace littéraire*. Paris: Gallimard, 1953.
———. "The Essential Solitude." In *The Space of Literature*, trans. Ann Smock, pp. 19–34. Lincoln: University of Nebraska Press, 1982.
———. *Friendship*. Trans. Elizabeth Rottenberg. Stanford, CA: Stanford University Press, 1997.
———. *The Infinite Conversation*. Trans. Susan Hanson. Minneapolis: University of Minnesota Press, 1993.
———. *The Last Man*. Trans. Lydia Davis. New York: Columbia University Press, 1987.
———. *Le pas au-delà*. Paris: Gallimard, 1973.
———. *The Space of Literature*. Trans. Ann Smock. Lincoln: University of Nebraska Press, 1982.
———. *The Step Not Beyond*. Trans. Lycette Nelson. Albany: SUNY Press, 1992.
———. *Thomas the Obscure*. Trans. Robert Lamberton. Barrytown, NY: Station Hill, 1988.
———. *The Writing of the Disaster*. Trans. Ann Smock. Lincoln: University of Nebraska Press, 1986.
Blanchot, Maurice / Jacques Derrida. *The Instant of My Death/Demeure: Fiction and Testimony*. Trans. Elizabeth Rottenberg. Stanford, CA: Stanford University Press, 2000.

Borch-Jacobsen, M. de, E. Michaud, and Jean-Luc Nancy, eds. *Hypnoses*. Paris: Galilée, 1984.

Bowen, Elizabeth, and Robert Stone. "'Making the Human' in Sartre's Unpublished Dialectical Ethics." In *Writing the Politics of Difference*, ed. Hugh Silverman, pp. 111–22. Albany: SUNY Press, 1991.

Braidotti, Rose. "Becoming Woman: Or, Sexual Difference Revisited." *Theory, Culture, & Society*, 20, no. 3 (2003): 43–64.

Braunstein, Néstor. "Desire and Jouissance in the Teaching of Lacan." In *The Cambridge Companion to Lacan*, ed. Jean-Michel Rabaté, pp. 99–112. Cambridge: Cambridge University Press, 2003.

Bruns, Gerald L. "Foucault's Modernism: Language, Poetry, and the Experience of Freedom." In *On the Anarchy of Poetry and Philosophy: A Guide for the Unruly*, pp. 57–58. New York: Fordham University Press, 2006.

———. "The Last Romantic: Stanley Cavell and the Writing of Philosophy." In *Tragic Thoughts at the End of Philosophy: Language, Literature, and Ethical Theory*, pp. 199–217. Evanston, IL: Northwestern University Press, 1999.

———. *Maurice Blanchot: The Refusal of Philosophy*. Baltimore: Johns Hopkins University Press, 1997.

Büchner, Georg. *Lenz*. Trans. Michael Hamburger. West Newbury, MA: Frontier, 1969.

Cadava, Eduardo, Peter Connor, and Jean-Luc Nancy, eds. *Who Comes After the Subject?* London: Routledge, 1991.

Calarco, Matthew. "Deconstruction Is Not Vegetarianism: Humanism, Subjectivity, and Animal Ethics." *Continental Philosophy Review*, 37, no. 2 (2004): 175–201.

Caputo, John D. *Against Ethics: Contributions to a Poetics of Obligation with Constant Reference to Deconstruction*. Bloomington: Indiana University Press, 1993.

Carroll, Noël. *The Philosophy of Horror; or, Paradoxes of the Heart*. New York: Routledge, 1990.

Cavalieri, Paola, and Peter Singer. *The Great Ape Project: Equality Beyond Humanity*. New York: St. Martin's, 1994.

Cavell, Stanley. *The Claim of Reason: Wittgenstein, Skepticism, Morality, and Tragedy*. New York: Oxford University Press, 1979.

———. *Conditions Handsome and Unhandsome: The Constitution of Emersonian Perfectionism*. Chicago: University of Chicago Press, 1990.

———. *In Quest of the Ordinary: Lines of Skepticism and Romanticism*. Chicago: University of Chicago Press, 1988.

———. "An Interview with Stanley Cavell." In *The Senses of Stanley Cavell*, ed. Richard Fleming and Michael Payne, pp. 21–72. Lewisburg, PA: Bucknell University Press, 1989.

———. *Philosophical Passages: Wittgenstein, Emerson, Austin, Derrida*. Oxford: Basil Blackwell, 1995.

———. *The Senses of Walden: An Expanded Edition*. San Francisco: North Point, 1981.
Cherry, Christopher. "Machines as Persons?" In *Human Beings*, ed. David Cockburn, pp. 11–35. Cambridge: Cambridge University Press, 1991.
Chrétien, Jean-Louis. *L'appel et la réponse*. Paris: Minuit, 1992.
Churchland, Patricia. *Neurophilosophy: Toward a Unified Science of the Mind/Brain*. Cambridge, MA: MIT Press, 1986.
Churchland, Paul. "Eliminative Materialism and the Propositional Attitude." *Journal of Philosophy*, 78, no. 2 (1981): 67–90.
Coetzee, J. M. *The Lives of Animals*. Princeton, NJ: Princeton University Press, 1999.
Cohen, Jeffrey Jerome. *Monster Theory: Reading Culture*. Minneapolis: University of Minnesota Press, 1996.
Connolly, William. "Beyond Good and Evil: The Ethical Sensibility of Michel Foucault." In *The Later Foucault*, ed. Jeremy Moss, pp. 108–28. London: Sage, 1988.
Critchley, Simon, and Peter Dews, eds. *Deconstructed Subjectivities*. Albany: SUNY Press, 1996.
Cros, Caroline, et al. *Orlan: Carnal Art*. Trans. Deke Dusinberre. Paris: Flammarion, 2004.
Dallmayr, Fred. "The Ontology of Freedom: Heidegger and Political Philosophy." In *Polis and Praxis: Exercises in Contemporary Political Theory*, pp. 102–32. Cambridge, MA: MIT Press, 1984.
Dawkins, Richard. "Gaps in the Mind." In *The Great Ape Project: Equality Beyond Humanity*, ed. Paola Cavalieri and Peter Singer, pp. 80–101. New York: St. Martin's, 1994.
Deleuze, Gilles. "Desire and Pleasure." In *Foucault and His Interlocutors*, ed. Arnold I. Davidson, pp. 183–94. Chicago: University of Chicago Press, 1997.
———. *Difference and Repetition*. Trans. Paul Patton. New York: Columbia University Press, 1994.
———. *Différence et repetition*. Paris: Presses Universitaires de France, 1968.
———. *Foucault*. Trans. Seán Hand. Minneapolis: University of Minnesota Press, 1986.
———. *Francis Bacon: The Logic of Sensation*. Trans. Daniel W. Smith. Minneapolis: University of Minnesota Press, 2003.
———. *The Logic of Sense*. Trans. Mark Lester. New York: Columbia University Press, 1990.
———. "Michel Tournier and the World Without Others." In *The Logic of Sense*, trans. Constantin Boundas, pp. 301–20. New York: Columbia University Press, 1990.
———. "One Manifesto Less." Trans. Alan Ornstein. In *The Deleuze Reader*, ed. Constantin Boundas, pp. 204–22. New York: Columbia University Press, 1993.
Deleuze, Gilles, and Félix Guattari. *Anti-Oedipus: Capitalism and Schizophrenia*. Trans. Robert Hurley, Mark Seem, and Helen R. Lane. Minneapolis: University of Minnesota Press, 1983.

———. *Kafka: Toward a Minor Literature.* Trans. Dana Polan. Minneapolis: University of Minnesota Press, 1986.

———. *Mille plateaux.* Paris: Minuit, 1980.

———. *A Thousand Plateaus.* Trans. Brian Massumi. Minneapolis: University of Minnesota Press, 1987.

———. *What Is Philosophy?* Trans. Hugh Tomlinson and Graham Burchell. New York: Columbia University Press, 1994.

Dennett, Daniel. *Brainstorms: Philosophical Essays on Mind and Psychology.* Cambridge, MA: MIT Press, 1981.

———. *Consciousness Explained.* Boston: Little, Brown, 1991.

———. *Content and Consciousness.* London: Routledge, 1993.

———. *Kinds of Minds: Toward an Understanding of Consciousness.* New York: Basic Books, 1996.

Derrida, Jacques. *L'animal autobiographique: Autour de Jacques Derrida.* Ed. Marie-Louise Mallet. Paris: Galilée, 1999.

———. *L'animal que donc je suis.* Ed. Marie-Louise Mallet. Paris: Galilée, 2006.

———. *The Animal That I Therefore Am.* Ed. Marie-Louise Mallet. Trans. David Wills. New York: Fordham University Press, 2008.

———. *Circonfession.* Paris: Éditions Seuil, 1991.

———. "'Eating Well,' or the Calculation of the Subject: An Interview with Jacques Derrida." In *Who Comes After the Subject?* ed. Eduardo Cadava, Peter Connor, and Jean-Luc Nancy, pp. 96–119. London: Routledge, 1991.

———. "The Ends of Man." In *Margins of Philosophy*, trans. Alan Bass, pp. 109–36. Chicago: University of Chicago Press, 1982.

———. "Geschlecht II: Heidegger's Hand." Trans. John P. Leavey. In *Deconstruction and Philosophy*, ed. John Sallis, pp. 161–96. Chicago: University of Chicago Press, 1987.

———. "Hostipitality." Trans Barry Stocker and Forbes Morlock. *Angelaki*, 5, no. 3 (2000): 3–18.

———. *Monolinguism of the Other; or, The Prosthesis of Origin.* Trans. Patrick Mensah. Stanford, CA: Stanford University Press, 1998.

———. *Of Grammatology.* Trans. Gayatri Spivak. Baltimore: Johns Hopkins University Press, 1976.

———. *Of Hospitality.* Trans. Rachel Bowlby. Stanford, CA: Stanford University Press, 2000.

———. *On the Name.* Trans. Thomas Dutoit. Stanford, CA: Stanford University Press, 1995.

———. *On Touching—Jean-Luc Nancy.* Trans. Christine Irizarry. Stanford, CA: Stanford University Press, 2005.

———. "A Silkworm of One's Own." Trans. Geoffrey Bennington. *Oxford Literary Review*, 18, nos. 1–2 (1997): 3–65.

———. *Writing and Difference*. Trans. Alan Bates. Chicago: University of Chicago Press, 1978.

Derrida, Jacques, and Maurizio Ferraris. *A Taste for the Secret*. Trans. Giacomo Donis. London: Polity, 2001.

Diamond, Cora. "The Importance of Being Human." In *Human Beings*, ed. David Cockburn, pp. 35–82. Cambridge: Cambridge University Press, 1991.

———. *The Realistic Spirit*. Cambridge, MA: MIT Press, 1981.

Diamond, Jared. *The Third Chimpanzee: The Evolution and the Future of the Human Animal*. New York: HarperCollins, 1992.

Douglas, Adam. *The Beast Within: A History of the Werewolf*. London: Chapmans, 1992.

Dragon, Jean-Jacques. "The Work of Alterity: Bataille and Lacan." *Diacritics*, 26, no. 2 (Summer 1996): 31–48.

Elden, Stuart. "Heidegger's Animals." *Continental Philosophy Review*, 39 (2006): 273–91.

Foucault, Michel. *Abnormal: Lectures at the Collège de France, 1974–1975*. Ed. Valerio Marchetti and Antonella Salomani. Trans. Graham Burchell. New York: Picador, 2003.

———. *L'archéologie du savoir*. Paris: Gallimard, 1969.

———. *The Archeology of Knowledge*. Trans. A. M. Sheridan Smith. New York: Harper & Row, 1972.

———. *The Birth of the Clinic: An Archeology of Medical Perception*. Trans. Alan Sheridan. New York: Vintage Books, 1975.

———. *Discipline and Punish: The Birth of the Prison*. Trans. Alan Sheridan. New York: Vintage Books, 1977.

———. *Dits et écrits, I: 1954–1976*. Ed. Daniel Defert and François Ewald. Paris: Gallimard, 2001.

———. *Dits et écrits, II: 1976–1988*. Ed. Daniel Defert and François Ewald. Paris: Gallimard, 2001.

———. *Essential Works of Foucault, 1954–1984*, vol. 1, *Ethics, Subjectivity, and Truth*. Ed. James D. Faubion. Trans. Robert Hurley et al. New York: New Press, 1997.

———. *Essential Works of Foucault: 1954–1984*, vol. 2, *Aesthetics, Method, and Epistemology*. Ed. James D. Faubion. Trans. Robert Hurley et al. New York: New Press, 1998.

———. *Essential Works of Michel Foucault, 1954–1984*, vol. 3, *Power*. Ed. James D. Faubion. Trans. Robert Hurley et al. New York: New Press, 1998.

———. *Folie et déraison: Histoire de la folie à l'âge classique*. Paris: Librairie Plon, 1961.

———. "For an Ethics of Discomfort." In *The Politics of Truth*, ed. Sylvère Lotringer and Lysa Hochroth, pp. 135–46. New York: Semiotext(e), 1997.

———. *Herculine Barbin: Being the Recently Discovered Memoirs of a Nineteenth-Century Hermaphrodite*. Trans. Richard McDougall. Introduction by Michel Foucault. New York: Pantheon Books, 1980.

———. *The Hermeneutics of the Subject: Lectures at the Collège de France, 1981–82*. Ed. Frédéric Gros. Trans. Graham Burchell. New York: Palgrave Macmillan, 2005.

———. *Histoire de la sexualité, I: La volonté de savoir*. Paris: Gallimard, 1984.

———. *Histoire de la sexualité, II: L'usage des plaisirs*. Paris: Gallimard, 1984.

———. *Histoire de la sexualité, III: Le souci de soi*. Paris: Gallimard, 1984.

———. *The History of Sexuality*, vol. 1, *An Introduction*. Trans. Robert Hurley. New York: Vintage Books, 1990.

———. *The History of Sexuality*, vol. 2, *The Uses of Pleasure*. Trans. Robert Hurley. New York: Vintage Books, 1990.

———. *The History of Sexuality*, vol. 3, *The Care of the Self*. Trans. Robert Hurley. New York: Random House, 1988.

———, ed. *I, Pierre Rivière, Having Slaughtered My Mother, My Sister and My Brother: A Case of Parricide in the 19th Century*. Trans. Frank Jellinek. Lincoln: University of Nebraska Press, 1975.

———. *Madness and Civilization: A History of Insanity in the Age of Reason*. Trans. Richard Howard. New York: Vintage Books, 1965.

———. *Naissance de la clinique*. Paris: Presses Universitaires de France, 1963.

———. *The Order of Things: An Archeology of the Human Sciences*. New York: Vintage Books, 1973.

———. *The Politics of Truth*. Ed. Sylvère Lotringer and Lysa Hochroth. New York: Semiotext(e), 1997.

———. *Surveiller et punir: Naissance de la prison*. Paris: Gallimard, 1975.

Foucault, Michel, and Maurice Blanchot. *Foucault/Blanchot*. Trans. Jeffrey Mehlman and Brian Massumi. New York: Zone Books, 1987.

Franck, Didier. *Chair et corps: Sur la phenomenologie de Husserl*. Paris: Minuit, 1981.

Frank, Manfred. "Is Subjectivity a Non-Thing, an Absurdity [*Unding*]? On Some Difficulties in Naturalistic Reductions of Self-Consciousness." In *The Modern Subject: Conceptions of the Self in Classical German Philosophy*, ed. Karl Ameriks and Dieter Sturma, pp. 177–97. Albany: SUNY Press, 1995.

———. *What Is Neostructuralism?* Trans. Sabine Wilke and Richard Gray. Minneapolis: University of Minnesota Press, 1989.

Freud, Sigmund. *Totem and Taboo: Some Points of Agreement Between the Mental Lives of Savages and Neurotics*. Trans. James Strachey. New York: W. W. Norton, 1950.

Frye, Northrop. *Anatomy of Criticism: Four Essays*. Princeton, NJ: Princeton University Press, 1957.

Goulmari, Pelagia. "A Minortarian Feminism? Things to Do with Deleuze and Guattari." *Hypatia*, 14, no. 2 (1999): 97–120.

Grosz, Elizabeth. "A Thousand Tiny Sexes: Feminism and Rhizomatics." *Topoi: An International Review of Philosophy*, 12, no. 2 (1993): 167–79.

Gutting, Gary, ed. *The Cambridge Companion to Foucault*. Cambridge: Cambridge University Press, 1994; 2nd ed., 2005.

———. "Foucault's Philosophy of Experience." *boundary 2*, 29, no. 2 (2002): 69–86.

Hacking, Ian. "Making Up People." In *Reconstructing Individualism: Autonomy, Individuality, and the Self in Western Thought*, ed. Thomas C. Heller, Morton Sosna, and David E. Wellbery, pp. 222–36. Stanford, CA: Stanford University Press, 1986.

Hadot, Pierre. *Philosophy as a Way of Life: Spiritual Exercises from Socrates to Foucault*. Trans. Michael Chase. Oxford: Basil Blackwell, 1995.

———. "Reflections on the Notion of 'the Cultivation of the Self.'" In *Michel Foucault: Philosopher*, trans. Timothy Armstrong, pp. 225–32. New York: Routledge, 1992.

Haraway, Donna. *Simians, Cyborgs, and Women: The Reinvention of Nature*. New York: Routledge, 1991.

Hayles, N. Katherine. *How We Became Posthuman: Virtual Bodies in Cybernetics, Literature, and Informatics*. Chicago: University of Chicago Press, 1999.

Hegel, Georg Wilhelm Friedrich. *The Phenomenology of Spirit*. Trans. A. V. Miller. Oxford: Oxford University Press, 1997.

Heidegger, Martin. *Being and Time*. Trans. John Macquarrie and Edward Robinson. New York: Harper & Row, 1962.

———. *Discourse on Thinking*. Trans. John Anderson and E. Hans Freund. New York: Harper & Row, 1966.

———. *Poetry, Language, Thought*. Trans. Albert Hofstadter. New York: Harper & Row, 1971.

———. *What Is Called Thinking?* Trans. J. Glenn Gray. New York: Harper & Row, 1968.

Hollis, Martin. *Models of Man: Philosophical Thoughts on Social Action*. Cambridge: Cambridge University Press, 1977.

Huffer, Lynn. "Foucault's Ethical *Ars Poetica*." *SubStance*, 38, no. 3 (2009): 129–47.

Ince, Kate. *Orlan: Millennial Female*. New York: Oxford University Press, 2000.

Janicaud, Dominique. *On the Human Condition*. Trans. Eileen Brennan. London: Routledge, 2005.

Jardine, Alice. "Women in Limbo: Deleuze and His Br(others)." *SubStance*, 13, nos. 2–3 (1984): 46–60.

Kafka, Franz. *The Complete Stories*. Trans. Nahum N. Glatzer. New York: Schocken Books, 1971.

———. *The Diaries: 1910–1922*. Ed. Max Brod. New York: Schocken Books, 1975.

Kierkegaard, Søren. *The Concept of Irony, with Constant Reference to Socrates*. Trans. Howard V. Hong and Edna H. Hong. Princeton, NJ: Princeton University Press, 1992.

Kojève, Alexander. *Introduction to the Reading of Hegel*. Trans. James H. Nichols, Jr. Ithaca, NY: Cornell University Press, 1980.

Kontos, Alkis. "The World Disenchanted." In *The Barbarism of Reason: Max Weber and the Twilight of Enlightenment*, ed. Asher Horowitz and Terry Maley, pp. 223–47. Toronto: University of Toronto Press, 1994.

Krell, David Farrell. "All You Can't Eat: Derrida's Course, 'Rhetorique du Cannibalisme' (1990–1991)." *Research in Phenomenology*, 36 (2006): 130–80.

Kristeva, Julia. "Bataille, Experience, and Practice." In *On Bataille: Critical Essays*, ed. Leslie Anne Boldt-Irons, pp. 237–64. Albany: SUNY Press, 1995.

———. *Powers of Horror: An Essay in Abjection*. New York: Columbia University Press, 1982.

Lacan, Jacques. *Écrits: A Selection*. Trans. Alan Sheridan. New York: W. W. Norton, 1977.

———. "The *Jouissance* of Transgression." In *The Ethics of Psychoanalysis*, trans. Dennis Porter, pp. 191–204. New York: W. W. Norton, 1992.

———. "The Wolf! The Wolf!" In *The Seminar of Jacques Lacan*, vol. 1, *Freud's Papers on Technique, 1953–54*, trans. John Forrester, pp. 86–106. New York: W. W. Norton, 1988.

Lecercle, Jean-Jacques. *Philosophy Through the Looking Glass: Language, Nonsense, Desire*. LaSalle, IL: Open Court, 1985.

Levinas, Emmanuel. *Autrement qu'être ou au-delà de l'essence*. The Hague: Martinus Nijhoff, 1974.

———. *Collected Philosophical Papers*. Trans. Alphonso Lingis. The Hague: Martinus Nijhoff, 1987.

———. *Difficult Freedom: Essays in Judaism*. Trans. Sean Hand. Baltimore: Johns Hopkins University Press, 1990.

———. *Of God Who Comes to Mind*. Trans. Bettina Bergo. Stanford, CA: Stanford University Press, 1998.

———. *Otherwise Than Being, or Beyond Essence*. Trans. Alphonso Lingis. The Hague: Martinus Nijhoff, 1971.

———. "The Rights of Man and the Rights of the Other." In *Outside the Subject*, trans. Michael Smith, pp. 116–34. Stanford, CA: Stanford University Press, 1994.

———. *Totalité et infini: Essai sur l'extériorité*. The Hague: Martinus Nijhoff, 1961.

———. *Totality and Infinity: An Essay on Exteriority*. Trans. Alphonso Lingis. Pittsburgh: Duquesne University Press, 1969.

Lyotard, Jean-François. *The Inhuman: Reflections on Time*. Trans. Geoffrey Bennington and Rachel Bowlby. Stanford, CA: Stanford University Press, 1991.

———. *Political Writings*. Trans. Bill Readings and Kevin Paul Geiman. Minneapolis: University of Minnesota Press, 1993.

Lysaker, John T. *Emerson and Self-Culture*. Bloomington: University of Indiana Press, 2008.

Mallet, Marie-Louise, ed. *L'animal autobiographique*. Paris: Galilée, 1999.

Marder, Michael. "Taming the Beast: The Other Tradition in Political Theory." *Mosaic*, 39, no. 4 (2006): 47–60.

Margolis, Joseph. *Texts Without Referents: Reconciling Science and Narrative*. Oxford: Basil Blackwell, 1989.

———. *Life Without Principles: Reconciling Theory and Practice*. Oxford: Basil Blackwell, 1996.

Mauss, Marcel. "A Category of the Human Mind: The Notion of the Person; the Notion of the Self." Trans. W. D. Halls. In *The Category of the Person: Anthropology, Philosophy, History*, ed. Michael Carruthers, Steven Collins, and Steven Lukes, pp. 1–25. Cambridge: Cambridge University Press, 1985.

May, Todd. *The Political Philosophy of Poststructuralist Anarchism*. University Park: Pennsylvania State University Press, 1994.

McCaffery, Steve. *North of Intention: Critical Writings, 1976–1982*. New York: ROOF Books, 1986.

Melehy, Hassan. "Silencing the Animals: Montaigne, Descartes, and the Hyperbole of Reason." *Symploke*, 13, nos. 1–2 (2005): 262–83.

Merleau-Ponty, Maurice. *The Visible and the Invisible*. Trans. Alphonso Lingis. Evanston, IL: Northwestern University Press, 1968.

Midgley, Mary. *Beast and Man: The Roots of Human Nature*. Rev. ed. London: Routledge, 1995.

Miller, James. *The Passion of Michel Foucault*. Cambridge, MA: Harvard University Press, 1993.

Moos, David. "Memories of Being: Orlan's Theater of the Self." *Art+Text*, 54 (1996): 67–72.

Musil, Robert. *The Man Without Qualities*. Trans. Eithne Wilkins and Ernst Kaiser. New York: G. P. Putnam's Sons, 1980.

Nancy, Jean-Luc. *Being Singular Plural*. Trans. Robert D. Richardson and Anne E. O'Byrne. Stanford, CA: Stanford University Press, 2000.

———. *The Birth to Presence*. Trans. Claudette Sartiliot. Stanford, CA: Stanford University Press, 1993.

———. *La communauté désœuvrée*. Paris: C. Bourgeois, 1990.

———. *Corpus*. Paris: Métailié, 1992.

———. *Être singulier pluriel*. Paris: Galilée, 1996.

———. *L'expérience de la liberté*. Paris: Galilée, 1988.

———. *The Experience of Freedom*. Trans. Bridget McDonald. Stanford, CA: Stanford University Press, 1993.

———. *The Fall of Sleep*. Trans. Charlotte Mandell. New York: Fordham University Press, 2009.

———. *The Inoperative Community*. Ed. Peter Connor. Trans. Peter Connor, Lisa Garbus, Michael Holland, and Simona Sawhney. Minneapolis: University of Minnesota Press, 1991.

———. *L'oubli de la philosophie*. Paris: Galilée, 1986.

———. *The Sense of the World*. Trans. Jeffrey S. Librett. Minneapolis: University of Minnesota Press, 1997.

———. *Tombe de sommeil*. Paris: Galilée, 2007.

Nietzsche, Friedrich. *Untimely Meditations*. Ed. Daniel Breazeale. Trans. R. J. Hollinsdale. Cambridge: Cambridge University Press, 1997.

Nussbaum, Martha. *The Fragility of Goodness: Luck and Ethics in Greek Tragedy and Philosophy*. Cambridge: Cambridge University Press, 1986.

———. *Frontiers of Justice: Disability, Nationality, Species Membership*. Cambridge, MA: Harvard University Press, 2006.

O'Bryan, C. Jill. *Carnal Art: Orlan's Refacing*. Minneapolis: University of Minnesota Press, 2005.

O'Leary, Timothy. "Foucault, Experience, Literature." *Foucault Studies*, no. 5 (January 2008): 5–25.

Otten, Charlotte F., ed. *The Lycanthropy Reader: Werewolves in Western Culture*. Syracuse, NY: Syracuse University Press, 1986.

Ovid. *Metamorphoses*. Trans. Mary M. Innes. London: Penguin Books, 1955.

Patton, Paul. "Conceptual Politics and the War-Machine in *Mille plateaux*." *SubStance*, 13, nos. 3–4 (1985): 61–80.

Piercy, Marge. *He, She, and It*. New York: Alfred Knopf, 1991.

Preston, Ted. "The Public and Private Appeal of Self-Fashioning." *Journal of Nietzsche Studies*, 3l (2006): 10–19.

Putnam, Hilary. "Robots: Machines or Artificially Created Life?" In *Mind, Language, and Reality*, pp. 386–408. Cambridge: Cambridge University Press, 1975.

Rapaport, Herman. *The Later Derrida: Reading the Recent Work*. London: Routledge, 2003.

Ricoeur, Paul. *Oneself as Another*. Trans. Kathleen Blamey. Chicago: University of Chicago Press, 1992.

Rilke, Rainer-Maria. *The Selected Poems of Rainer Maria Rilke*. Trans. Stephen Mitchell. New York: Vintage Books, 1982.

Rorty, Richard. *Contingency, Irony, and Solidarity*. Cambridge: Cambridge University Press, 1989.

Rose, Barbara. "Is It Art? Orlan and the Transgressive Act." *Art in America*, 81, no. 2 (1993): 82–89.

Sartre, Jean-Paul. *Being and Nothingness*. Trans. Hazel Barnes. New York: Washington Square, 1956.

———. "Existentialism Is a Humanism." In *Existentialism from Dostoevsky to Sartre*, ed. Walter Kaufmann, pp. 345–68. New York: Meridian Books, 1959.

Sass, Louis A. "Humanism, Hermeneutics, and the Concept of the Human Subject." In *Hermeneutics and Psychological Theory: Interpretive Perspectives on Personality, Psychotherapy, and Psychopathology*, ed. Stanley B. Messer, Louis A. Sass, and Robert L. Woolfolk, pp. 222–71. New Brunswick, NJ: Rutgers University Press, 1988.

Scarry, Elaine. *The Body in Pain: The Making and Unmaking of the World*. New York: Oxford University Press, 1985.

Schlegel, Friedrich. *Philosophical Fragments*. Trans. Peter Firchow. Minneapolis: University of Minnesota Press, 1991.

Schmiedel, Stevie. "With or Without Lacan? Becoming-Woman Between the Language of Organs and the Anorganism of Language." *theory@buffalo*, no. 8: "Deleuze and Feminism" (2003): 11–41.

Seppä, Anita. "Foucault, Enlightenment, and the Aesthetics of the Self." *Contemporary Aesthetics*, 2 (2004): www.contempaesthetics.org/newvolume/pages/article.php?articleID=244.

Serres, Michel. *Genesis*. Trans. Geneviève James and James Nielson. Ann Arbor: University of Michigan Press, 1995.

———. *The Parasite*. Trans. Lawrence R. Schehr. Baltimore: Johns Hopkins University Press, 1982.

Simmel, Georg. "The Metropolis and Mental Life." In *On Individuality and Social Forms*, trans. Donald E. Levine, pp. 324–29. Chicago: University of Chicago Press, 1971.

Sloterdijk, Peter. "Rules for the Human Zoo: A Response to the *Letter on Humanism*." Trans. Mary Varney Rorty. *Environment and Planning D: Space and Society*, 27 (2009): 12–28.

Stein, Gertrude. *Gertrude Stein: Writings and Lectures, 1909–1945*. Trans. Patricia Meyerowitz. London: Penguin Books, 1967.

Stich, Steven. *From Folk Psychology to Cognitive Science*. Cambridge, MA: MIT Press, 1983.

Sunstein, Cass R., and Martha Nussbaum. *Animal Rights: Current Debates and New Directions*. Oxford: Oxford University Press, 2004.

Sylvester, David. *The Brutality of Fact: Interviews with Francis Bacon, 1962–1979*. New York: Thames and Hudson, 1987.

Tournier, Michel. *Friday*. Trans. Norman Denny. New York: Pantheon Books, 1969.

———. *Vendredi, ou les limbes du Pacifique*. Paris: Gallimard, 1967.

Tyler, Tom. "Deviants, Donestre, and Debauchees: Here Be Monsters." *Culture, Theory, & Critique*, 49, no. 2 (2008): 113–31.

———. "Four Hands Good, Two Hands Bad." *Parallax*, 12, no. 1 (2006): 69–80.

Ure, Michael. "Senecan Moods: Foucault and Nietzsche on the Art of the Self." *Foucault Studies*, no. 4 (February 2007), 20–28.

Valéry, Paul. *Selected Writings of Paul Valéry*. Trans. Denis Devlin et al. New York: New Directions, 1950.

Veyne, Paul. "The Final Foucault and His Ethics." In *Foucault and His Interlocutors*, ed. Arnold Davidson, pp. 225–33. Chicago: University of Chicago Press, 1997.

Villiers de l'Isle-Adam, Auguste. *Tomorrow's Eve*. Trans. Robert Martin Adams. Urbana: University of Illinois Press, 1982.

Wegenstein, Bernadette. "Getting Under the Skin; or, How Faces Have Become Obsolete." *Configurations*, 10 (2003): 221–59.

Wilkes, Kathleen. *Real People: Personal Identity Without Thought Experiments*. Oxford: Clarendon Press, 1988.

Williams, Bernard. *Making Sense of Humanity and Other Philosophical Papers*. Cambridge: Cambridge University Press, 1995.
Wittgenstein, Ludwig. *Philosophical Investigations*. Trans. G. E. M. Anscombe. New York: Macmillan, 1953.
———. *Tractatus Logico-Philosophicus*. Trans. D. F. Pears and B. F. McGuinness. London: Routledge & Kegan Paul, 1961.
Wolfe, Cary. 2003. *Animal Rites: American Culture, the Discourse of Species, and Posthumanist Theory*. Chicago: University of Chicago Press, 2003.
———. "In the Shadow of Wittgenstein's Lion: Language, Ethics, and the Question of the Animal." In *Zoontologies: The Question of the Animal*, ed. Cary Wolfe, pp. 1–57. Minneapolis: University of Minnesota Press, 2004.
———, ed. *Zoontologies: The Question of the Animal*. Minneapolis: University of Minnesota Press, 2004.
Zeitlin, Froma. "Playing the Other: Theater, Theatricality, and the Feminine in Greek Drama." *Representations*, 11 (1985): 63–94; reprinted in *Playing the Other: Gender and Society in Classical Greek Literature*, pp. 341–74. Chicago: University of Chicago Press, 1996.

Index

Aaltola, Elise, 75–76
Adams, Parveen, 70
Adorno, Theodor W., *Aesthetic Theory*, 50, 100n14, 103n20; "Vers une musique informel," 7–8
Agamben, Giorgio, *Homo Sacer*, 23, 33, 41, 44, 86; *Infancy and History*, 86–87, 114–15n15; *Man Without Content*, 51; *The Open*, 46, 73
alterity (*Autrui*), 2, 15–16, 24, 29, 34, 64, 82, 84–85, 99n5, 100n13, 100n15
animals, 42–43, 75–77, 83–92
anomaly, 32, 63–64

"bare life," 23, 25, 41, 65, 86, 106n43
Bataille, Georges, "Celestial Bodies," 60; on the festival, 67; "Hegel, Death, and Sacrifice," 59; on the heterogeneous, 65–66; *Inner Experience*, 47, 56–57, 59, 86; on the "me," 99n7; "Notion of Expenditure," 60, 67, 114n10; "Practice of Joy Before Death," 59–60; "Preface" to *Madame Edwarda*, 60; "Psychological Structure of Fascism," 112n3; "Sovereignty," 28, 49–50
Blanchot, Maurice, "Essential Solitude," 1–3, 99n1; *Friendship*, 95, 116n3; *Infinite Conversation*, 56–57, 64, 84–85, 95; "Instant of My Death," 112n26; "Last Man," 56, 111n20; "Limit-Experience," 117n8; "Michel Foucault as I Remember Him," 50; "Relation of the Third Kind," 1–2, 48, 84–85, 110n3; *Step Not Beyond*, 2, 107n2; *Thomas the Obscure*, 108n12; *Writing of the Disaster*, 2, 86
Body without Organs, 67–69, 74
Burden, Chris, 70

Cavell, Stanley, *Claim of Reason*, 14, 32, 36–37, 41–45, 105n28; *Conditions Handsome and Unhandsome*, 18–19, 105n31
Cherry, Christopher, 15
child, 27–29, 85–87, 107n3
Coetzee, J. M., *Lives of Animals*, 76, 89
cyborg, 13, 74–75, 109n21

Deleuze, Gilles, *Difference and Repetition*, 48–50; *Foucault*, 50; *Francis Bacon*, 71–73; *Logic of Sense*, 62; "Michel Tournier and the World Without Others," 106–7n44
Deleuze, Gilles, and Felix Guattari, *Anti-Oedipus*, 67–70; *Kafka: Toward a Minor Literature*, 37, 62–63; *Thousand Plateaus*, 61–67, 72–76
Dennett, Daniel, *Consciousness Explained*, 14, 102n8, 109n15; *Content and Consciousness*, 102n5; *Kinds of Minds*, 15
Derrida, Jacques, "And Say the Animal Responded," 85; "Animal that I Therefore Am," 79–97; "Eating Well," 87–88, 116n3; "Ends of Man," 91; "From Restricted to General Economy," 107n46; *Monolingualism of the Other*, 96; *Taste for the Secret*, 79, 82, 95–96

Diamond, Cora, "Eating Meat and Eating People," 91–92; "Importance of Being Human," 13–14
Diamond, Jared, 109n16
difference, 11, 47–48, 73, 81, 92, 110n6

face, 70–73, 115n17; face-to-face, 17, 15, 72, 83–84
fellow creatures, 44, 75–77, 90–92
first-person, 37–39, 48–49, 54, 56, 111n21
flesh, 16–17, 41–43, 65–68, 71–73, 81, 113n8, 113–14n9
Foucault, Michel, *Abnormal*, 53; "Ethics of the Concern of the Self as a Practice of Freedom," 50; "For an Ethics of Discomfort," 50; *History of Sexuality*, 20, 47, 51–54, 58–59; "Interview with Michel Foucault" (1980), 57–58; "Introduction" to *Herculin Barbin*, 55–56; "Lives of Infamous Men," 55; *Madness and Civilization*, 54; "Masked Philosopher," 50–51; "Maurice Florence," 47; "On the Genealogy of Ethics," 20, 48; *Order of Things*, 13; "Preface to the *History of Sexuality*, v. 2*," 53; "Preface to Transgression," 56; "Thought of the Outside," 56; "What Is Enlightenment?" 20
Frank, Manfred, 21
Freud, Sigmund, *Totem and Taboo*, 107n3
freedom, 1–2, 4–8, 28, 50, 56, 58–60, 82, 96–97, 99n11, 100n12
Frye, Northrop, 36

Hacking, Ian, 75, 101n4
Hadot, Pierre, 59, 111n22
Haraway, Donna, 13–17
Hegel, Georg Wilhelm Friedrich, 5–6, *Phenomenology of Spirit*, 49
Heidegger, Martin, "The Origin of the Work of Art," 100n12; *What Is Called Thinking?* 83–84, 116–17n6
heterogeneous, 65–66, 112n3
Hollis, Martin, *Models of Man*, 18, 105n28
homo sacer, 33–34
horror, 43–44, 109.19

identity/non-identity, 1–5, 21–22, 28, 43, 48–51, 55–57, 73, 95–97, 100n14, 111n20

Kafka, Franz, "Burrow," 39; *Diaries*, 39, 108n11; "Metamorphosis," 37–39; "Report to the Academy," 39–41, 43–44
Kojève, Alexandre, *Introduction to the Reading of Hegel*, 14–15, 112n29, 112–13n6
Kristeva, Julia, *Powers of Horror*, 65–66

Lacan, Jacques, "The Freudian Thing," 38; "*Jouissance* of Transgression," 59, 112n24; "Mirror Phase," 117n5; "The Wolf! The Wolf!" 107n3
language, 61, 70, 86–88, 117n11
Levinas, Emmanuel. "Bad Conscience and the Inexorable," 22; *Difficult Freedom*, 92–94; "Humanism and Anarchy," 16; *Otherwise than Being*, 3, 16–18, 22–23; "Rights of Man," 15–16; "Signature," 18; "Substitution," 2–3; *Totality and Infinity*, 84–85, 99n1
limit-experience, 1, 43, 47, 56–60, 69–70, 85–86, 117n8
Lyotard, François, "After Wittgenstein," 13; *Inhuman*, 13, 27–28

machine, 15, 41, 45–46, 91, 115n20
Margolis, Joseph, *Life Without Principles*,

101n4; *Texts Without Referents*, 38, 102n5, 104n22

Mauss, Marcel, 105n30 (on *personne v. moi*)

me (*moi*), 3–4, 16–17, 21–22, 35, 37, 48, 99n7, 105n30

Merleau-Ponty, Marcel, *Visible and Invisible*, 115–16n9 (on "flesh")

metamorphosis, 24, 32, 37–38, 50, 62–63, 107n5, 108n12

Midgley, Mary, "The Beast Within," 103n14

molar/molecular combinations, 61, 68, 73–74

Musil, Robert, *Man Without Qualities*, 36

Nancy, Jean-Luc, *Being Singular Plural*, 9, 110n6; *Birth to Presence*, 68, 99n10; "Corpus," 113n8; *Experience of Freedom*, 6–7, 99n11; *Fall of Sleep*, 3–10; *Inoperative Community*, 10, 60, 100–101n15; *Sense of the World*, 100n3

neuter, 1–3, 56–57

Nietzsche, Friedrich, 20, 47

no one, 1–3, 22, 56, 86, 99n1, 103n19, 105n30

Nussbaum, Martha, 91, 102n9

Orlan, 70–71

Ovid, 31–34

persons, 75–76

Piercy, Marge, *He, She, It*, 103n16, 109n21

Plato, 14, 16, 103.19

Putnam, Hilary, 15

Rapaport, Herman, 80

Ricoeur, Paul, *Oneself as Another*, 106n42

Rilke, Rainer-Marie, "Schwartz-Katze," 83

Rorty, Richard, 20

Sartre, Jean-Paul, *Being and Nothingness*, 17, 19–20, 79–80, 105–6n33; "Existentialism Is a Humanism, 20

Scarry, Elaine, 107–8n5

Schlegel, Friedrich, *Philosophical Fragments*, 106n38

self, 2–4, 17–20, 22–23, 48, 53, 57–60, 79–80

Serres, Michel, *Genesis*, 114n13; *Parasite*, 108–9n12

Simmel, Georg, "Metropolis and Mental Life," 108n9

singularity, 2, 6–7, 10–11, 22, 49, 82–84, 100n13, 100–101n15

sleep, 3–8

Sloterdijk, Peter, "Rules for the Human Zoo," 52

Smuts, Barbara, 76–77

sovereignty, 28, 52, 60, 107n46

subjectivity, 3–5, 16, 18, 21–23, 47–48, 50, 84, 104n23

theater of cruelty, 69–71

Tournier, Michel, *Friday*, 23–29, 60, 106n44

Valéry, Paul, 113n8 (on "three bodies")

Villiers de l'Isle-Adam, *Tomorrow's Eve*, 45–46

werewolf, 33–34, 107n3

who, 3–4, 16, 79–83, 92, 94–97

Wilkes, Kathleen, *Real People*, 115n17 (on "pigs")

Wittgenstein, Ludwig, *Philosophical Investigations*, 38, *Tractatus Logico-Philosophicus*, 103.9